FOUR PRECURSORS OF
HENRY GEORGE

FOREWORDS

Ye may heed it not, ye haughty ones,
Whose hearts, like rocks, are cold ;
But the day will come when the fiat of God
In thunder shall be told ;
For the voice of the Great I AM hath said
That the land shall NOT be sold.

Gradually but surely has the separation been taking place between the privileged Landowner and the unprivileged Labourer.

And the time will come at last when there shall be but two parties looking each other in the face, and knowing that the destruction of the one is an event of necessary consequence. That event *must* come. Nor is it in man to stay it or produce it. It will come as the result of the laws that govern nature and govern man.

Of the two parties one must give way, one must sink to rise no more ; one must disappear from the earth. Their continued existence is incompatible. Nature cannot support both.—PATRICK E. DOVE : *Theory of Progression* (1850).

CONCERNING

FOUR PRECURSORS

OF

HENRY GEORGE

AND THE SINGLE TAX

AS ALSO

THE LAND GOSPEL

ACCORDING TO

WINSTANLEY "THE DIGGER"

BY

J. MORRISON DAVIDSON

KENNIKAT PRESS
Port Washington, N. Y./London

FOUR PRECURSORS OF HENRY GEORGE

First published in 1899
Reissued in 1971 by Kennikat Press
Library of Congress Catalog Card No: 77-115317
ISBN 0-8046-1108-4

Manufactured by Taylor Publishing Company   Dallas, Texas

TO

THE DISINHERITED LANDLESS HELOTS

OF

TOWN AND COUNTRY

AT

HOME AND ABROAD

THIS SMALL BUT PRECIOUS COMPENDIUM

OF

IMPERISHABLE TRUTHS

ON

THE LAND PROBLEM

IS

WITH THE DEEPEST SYMPATHY INSCRIBED BY

J. M. D.

COMMON ROOM, MIDDLE TEMPEL,
LONDON, *Nov.* 10, 1899

CONTENTS

FOUR PRECURSORS OF HENRY GEORGE

WILLIAM OGILVIE

THE EUCLID OF LAND LAW REFORM (1782)

"The Land shall not be sold in perpetuity; for the Land is Mine, saith the Lord."—*Leviticus.*

"Woe unto them that join house to house and lay field to field, till there be no place, that they may be placed alone in the midst of the Earth."—*Isaiah.*

"Cain was the first man in the world who divided the Common Property in the Earth by enclosures and landmarks."—*Josephus.*

"The notion of selling for certain bits of metal the Iliad of Homer, how much more the Land of the World-Creator, is a ridiculous impossibility."—*Carlyle.*

"The Land Question is the Bottom Question: Man is a Land Animal."—*Henry George.*

THE very first day the "Prophet of San Francisco" set foot in London, in the fall of 1881, I had the good fortune to encounter him in Fleet Street, and in the famous "Old Cheshire Cheese" we dined together, and before we parted I was in full possession of whatever is of abiding value in "Progress and Poverty."

In most cases of brilliant authorship the writer is markedly inferior to his literary offspring; but this could not be said of Henry George.   In truth, I much preferred the man to his book, the after-perusal of which that afternoon's lucid *vivâ voce* exposition rendered tame and unconvincing by comparison.

Indeed " Progress and Poverty " appeared in the very nick of time; otherwise it could never have attained a tithe of its phenomenal popularity. It was the terrible object-lesson of Ireland writhing in the grasp of a relentless landlordism that gave it nine-tenths of its significance.   The Hour had brought the Man.   The two were like hand and glove.

But it is a commonplace of history for the Man to come *before* his Hour, and then he is generally in an evil case.   The powers that be either deal summarily with him as a dangerous innovator, or ignore him as a harmless lunatic.   If he is not devoured by the Inquisition he is swallowed up by Oblivion.

Henry George had at least five remarkable precursors in this country, who fully grasped the realities of the Land Problem; to wit, Jerrard Win-

stanley, Thomas Spence, Thomas Paine, William
Ogilvie, and Patrick Edward Dove—all men worthy
of statues of the choicest marble in the grand
Temple of Humanity.

Of the first of these, Winstanley ("The Digger"),
I have sorrowfully to regret my total inability to
discover almost anything of his life-story. And
yet was he not merely a thinker of unusual pene-
tration and foresight in Commonwealth times, but
a fairly voluminous writer, and even a public
character, who raided the country with "Red
Vans," occasionally collided with the Fairfaxes
and other Parliamentarians, and courageously
lectured Old Noll himself.

Winstanley's solution of the Land Problem, as
will be seen, differs *toto cœlo* from that of Henry
George. It makes a clean sweep of "Sale and
Purchase, Rent and Money." It is Communism
pure and simple. First in time it is last in order.

But, for the present, my business is with a very
different sort of personage, Professor William
Ogilvie, of King's College, Old Aberdeen, my own
Alma Mater. He was a contemporary of Paine
and Spence, and his singularly logical and conclusive "Essay on Property in Land" bears date,

"London, 1782." The Essay was published anonymously, and the author's identity, in his own day, was a well-kept secret, except to a small circle of intimate friends. The "George Campaign" in Scotland, however, led to its disinterment in the Granite City, and ultimate republication in 1891, "With Biographical Notes by D. C. Macdonald" (Kegan Paul, Trench, Trübner & Co.), which leave no doubt whatever as to the authorship.

Yet, on the whole, despite Mr. Macdonald's unsparing research, Ogilvie, like Winstanley, remains, in a great measure, a "dark horse"; albeit he occupied a professorial Chair for the long period of fifty-four years, and was, beyond all question, one of the sanest intellects and most elegant scholars of his day. His death was barely noted in Scotland; but the *Times* (Feb. 23, 1819) records:—

" Mr. Ogilvie was one of the most accomplished scholars of the age. His talents were of the first order. His taste was of the most refined and correct nature, and the whole of his very prolonged life (eighty-three years) was passed in the ardent pursuit of knowledge. He died universally admired for his valuable acquirements, and esteemed by

all who knew him in private life for the benevolence of his heart, and the faithful discharge of
every social duty."

William Ogilvie, the only son of James Ogilvie,
Laird of Pittensear, Morayshire, and of Marjory
Steuart of Tannachy, Banffshire, was a patrician
born and bred. There were no fewer than three
earldoms among the Ogilvies—Airlie, Findlater,
and Seafield—the Pittensear family belonging to
the Findlater branch.

There is no authentic account of the boyhood
of the "Euclid of Land-Law Reform," but it is
reasonably assumed that it was spent at the man-
sion-house of Pittensear, and that he attended the
Grammar-School of Elgin, three miles off. At the
age of nineteen he entered King's College, Aberdeen, 1755–56, as third bursar, and graduated in
1759, when he was appointed Master of the
Grammar-School of Cullen. At Cullen he remained for but one year.

In 1760–61 we find him at Glasgow University,
studying under Dr. Joseph Black, of "Latent Heat
and Specific Heat" renown, at the very time that
James Watt, in his little workshop in the College
Buildings, was revolutionising the whole world of

industrial production, and he of the "Wealth of Nations" was learnedly prelecting from the Chair of Moral Philosophy.

In the following academic year (1761–62) Ogilvie attended the lectures of the Edinburgh Professors, and doubtless profited, there being then among the latter men of such mark as Dr. Blair, of "Rhetoric" and " Belles Lettres" fame ; Dr. Adam Ferguson, the historian ; and Dr. Cullen, the first man in Britain systematically to teach chemistry as a science.

In 1761, through the good offices of his kinsman, the Earl of Findlater and Seafield, Ogilvie secured a Chair in his Aberdeen *Alma Mater,* and became " Professor of Humanity (Latin Language and Literature) and Lecturer on Political and Natural History, Antiquities, Criticism, and Rhetoric "— a large enough order, it will be admitted, even for " the most accomplished scholar of the age." He acted, moreover, as travelling tutor and companion to Alexander, fourth Duke of Gordon, and in that capacity he probably himself acquired abroad as much knowledge as he imparted. He never encumbered himself with the impediment of a wife or child, his benevolence concerning itself with the welfare of the entire human family.

Strange to say, of all countries—and he cites most—he is silent about his own—Scotland. This, however, was part of his policy of anonymity. Scotland was then groaning under a despotism of the most crushing and flagitious order, and, except by insinuation or suggestion, there was no hope whatever of redress. The parliamentary electorate, all told, consisted of 2652 (!) souls, and landlordism ruled in Church and State with a rod of iron. Says Mr. Macdonald in his "Biographical Notes":—

"The State Church, although based on demo-cratic (Presbyterian) lines, approved of (Judge) Braxfield's doings. It issued a 'Pastoral Admoni-tion' in 1799 against Sunday-schools, and de-scribed the teachers as 'notoriously disaffected to the civil constitution of the country.' Thomas Muir, of Huntershill, an eminent Edinburgh advo-cate, had a copy of Paine's 'Rights of Man' in his possession, and this was made the principal *crime* for which he was banished (for fourteen years). Burns, in order to escape a similar fate, had to hide his copy and the 'Age of Reason' with the blacksmith of Dumfries. Professor Ogilvie's works would be considered more criminal than these. The man who dared to deny the divine origin of

rents and *tithes,* and, moreover, boldly defined
them as 'the improvident regulations of *human*
law,' and who was able to cite Moses as his authority, would doubtless be considered more dangerous
than the renowned Thomas Paine. It was perhaps on this account that no shelf could be found
in the Aberdeen University Library for a copy of
'The Rights of Property in Land,' while 'The
Rights of Man' did find a place in that conse-
crated ground. One of the books which Professor
Ogilvie had beside him when he died was the
University Library copy of 'The Rights of Man,'
and it is not improbable that the very last stroke
of his pen was employed in reviewing that book,
or in revising a new work on 'The Rights of Man
to the Land—how Lost, and how to be Regained.'"

That Ogilvie contemplated (and most probably
executed) an exhaustive "History of Property in
Land" we know on his own authority, and it is
not impossible that the invaluable MS. may yet be
unearthed, along with certain Horatian and Vir-
gilian translations, which competent judges pronounced of unrivalled excellence. Shortly after
his death the whole of his MSS. were "nailed up
in six or eight large boxes," to await the arrival of

one of his nephews, James Ogilvie Tod, an Indian judge, who was believed to have his uncle's instructions regarding their disposal. Did Tod wickedly and feloniously cremate them, or do they exist? They were, I understand, taken to Edinburgh.

But now to give the reader some notion of the cold Euclidian method of reasoning employed by Ogilvie in his "Rights of Property in Land," so strangely in contrast to the fervent periods of George's "Progress and Poverty." There is not to be found anywhere a finer illustration of applied logic. The "Essay" is divided into seventy-five numbered paragraphs, and the pith of each of these is most skilfully condensed in the "Contents." Thus :—

Ogilvie's Method of Analysis.

1. Each individual derives from the right of general occupancy a right to an equal share of the soil.

2. This right cannot be precluded by any possession of others.

3. Nor is it tacitly renounced by those who have no opportunity of entering upon it.

4. The opportunity of claiming this right ought to be reserved for every citizen.

5. Rude societies have respected this right; in the progress of the arts it is overlooked, and by conquests generally subverted.

6. Speculative reasoners have confounded this equal right with that which is founded in labour and ascertained by municipal laws.

7. The right of a landholder to an extensive estate must be founded chiefly in labour.

8. The progress of cultivation gives an ascendant to the right of labour over that of general occupancy.

9. But the public good requires that both should be respected and combined together.

10. Such combination is difficult, and has rarely been established for any length of time.

11. It is the proper object of Agrarian Laws, and effectual means of establishing it may be devised.

Paragraphs 12, 13, and 14 are most important, and may be thus abridged—

12. When a piece of land is sold, the price paid by the purchaser may be considered as

consisting of three parts, each being the value of a distinct subject, the separate amount of which men skilled in agriculture, and acquainted with the soil of the country, might accurately enough appreciate.

These " parts " are—

(*a*) The *original* value of the soil, or that which it might have borne in its natural state prior to all cultivation.

(*b*) The *accessory* or *improved* value of the soil, that, to wit, which it has received from the improvements and cultivation bestowed on it by the last proprietor and those who have preceded him.

(*c*) The *contingent* or *improvable* value of the soil ; that further value which it may still receive from future cultivation and improvements, over and above the expense of making such improvements, or, as it may be otherwise expressed, the value of exclusive right to make such improvements.

If, in England, 100 acres of arable land are sold for £1500, the *contingent* value may be reckoned at £500, *original* value at £200, and *accessory* or *improved* value at £800. In this example these three parts of the general value are to one another as 2, 8, and 5. If from 100 acres of uncultivated moorland in Ireland, the proportion of the parts may be as 1, 0, and 14.

13. The landholder must be allowed to have a full and absolute right to the *original,* the *improved,* and the *contingent* value of such portion of his estate as would fall to his share on an equal partition of the territory of the State among the citizens. Over the surplus extent of his estate he has a full right to the *accessory* value. But to the *original* and *contingent* value of this surplus extent he has no full right. That must *reside in the community at large,* and, though seemingly neglected or relinquished, may be claimed at pleasure by the Legislature, or by the magistrate who is the public trustee.

14. The *original* value of the soil is treated as a fund belonging to the public, and merely deposited in the hands of great proprietors, to be, by the imposition of land taxes, gradually applied to the public use, *until the whole be exhausted.*

Equity, however, requires that from such land

taxes those small tenements which do not exceed
the proprietor's natural share of the soil should be
exempted.

To separate the *contingent* value from the other
two is less difficult and of more importance; for
the detriment which the public suffers by neglect-
ing this separation, and permitting an exclusive
right of improving the soil to accumulate in the
hands of a small part of the community, is far
greater in respect both of the progress of agriculture and the comfortable independence of the
lower ranks.

It will thus be seen that though Ogilvie was a
Single Taxer of the most uncompromising character, he was careful to exempt "small tenements
which do not exceed the proprietor's *natural share*
of the soil." Consequently, if no one were permitted to exceed his "natural share," the Single
Tax would yield nothing. That is to say, the
Single Tax affords a tolerably drastic redress of
an intolerable injustice and inveterate evil, and
is not, as the Georgeans would have us believe,
a positive good *per se.*

But so long, for example, as in this London of

ours the Westminsters, Bedfords, Portmans, Port-
lands, and other ground-rent bandits exceed their
"natural shares" by £20,000,000 per annum, it
boots not to split hairs.   Let us rather, now and
always, pay grateful homage to the prophets of
Pittensear, San Francisco, or elsewhere, who have
at any time proclaimed, or shall proclaim, the
cardinal truth :

THE LAND QUESTION IS THE BOTTOM QUESTION :
MAN IS A LAND ANIMAL.

William Ogilvie lies buried in the south transept
of St. Machar's Cathedral, Old Aberdeen, where a
tablet in the wall, of very modest dimensions, describes him as " William Ogilvie, Esquire of Pittensear, in the County of Moray, and Professor of
Humanity in the University and King's College,
Aberdeen, who died on the 14th February, 1819,
aged 83 years."

When a student of King's, with its unique and
striking architectural crown, nearly forty years
ago, I remember noting this tablet, and wonder-
ing how it came, or *could* come, to pass that the
Laird of Pittensear ever rose, or fell, to fill the
Chair of Humanity.   Though then, necessarily, a

very young observer of social phenomena, I had a clear enough conviction that landlords, generally, are persons licensed to rob and oppress their fellow-mortals in sheer defiance of every principle of natural justice. But what would have been my amazement had any one told me—there was none to tell me, for the professors in my day were gerund-grinders of the most conventional and soulless type—that this forgotten landlord-professor was not merely a Humanist of the first order, but the very Euclid of the Rights of Man to the Land ?—a master of applied logic in no way inferior to the very greatest of his contemporaries, to Adam Smith, David Hume, Priestley, Paine, Franklin, or Condorcet.

The actual circumstances attending the suppression (for suppressed it must have been) of Ogilvie's " Rights of Property in Land " are not known ; but, as has been already said, there is no doubt as to the authorship. Among some of Ogilvie's private papers recently recovered the discharged account for printing the work has turned up, dated August 25th, 1781, and with it the following letter from his friend, Professor Thomas Reid, he of " Common Sense Philosophy " repute, and author of "An Inquiry into the Human Mind," Adam Smith's successor in the Chair of Moral Philosophy in the University of Glasgow. Reid's letter runs :—

"GLASGOW COLLEGE, *April* 7, 1789.

"DEAR SIR,—The bearer, Mr. George Gordon, a preacher, wished very much to be introduced to you. As he has been long of my acquaintance, and a young man whom I esteem, I could not refuse him that favour. He is much pleased with ' An Essay on Landed Property,' and cannot see a reason (neither can I) why it should go about like a foundling without its father's name. Men seem by degrees to improve in the notion of Liberty, and I hope will in that of *Property*. But though this earthly globe should be monopolised by a few to the exclusion of others, I hope the intellectual globe will always be *common*, and that those who possess the largest share will be still ready to impart to such as are willing to improve it. The bearer professes to belong to this last category, and hopes to increase his stock by a visit to Aberdeen.—I am, with much esteem and affection, dear sir, your very humble servant,

"THOMAS REID."

Yet Ogilvie was by no means indifferent to the fate of the "foundling." In a touching MS., dated Pittensear, September 12th, 1776, when, at 40, his health seemed completely shattered by over-study, Ogilvie implores "that Sovereign Power from whom I have received so many good gifts that some time may be allowed for the settlement of the affairs I leave behind me, and, if possible, to reduce into some form a synopsis at least of those contemplations and schemes which have occurred at various times to my mind, as of importance to the general welfare of mankind and the improvement of their present state."

Again, in the "Introduction" to his splendidly-reasoned treatise, the Prophet of Pittensear tells us that "the leading principles of that system, which he now holds, respecting property in land, have been coeval in his mind with the free exercise of his thoughts in speculative inquiries; they have recurred often, they have been gradually unfolded, and for some years past he has been accustomed to review them frequently, almost in their present form, and with still increasing approbation."

Nay, steps were cautiously taken to secure for

the "system" the approbation of such potent and diverse men of affairs as Frederick the Great of Prussia, George Washington in America, and Cornwallis in India. In the repositories of the Prussian Autocrat was found, significantly enough in the light of the sweeping land tenure reforms afterwards achieved by Stein and Hardenberg, a copy of Ogilvie's work, "with the author's compliments."

Indeed, our author was far more of a "practical politician" than, for example, his eminent pupil and loyal friend, Sir James Mackintosh, who wrote concerning him : " This most ingenious and accomplished recluse published without his name ' An Essay on the Right of Property in Land,' full of benevolence and ingenuity, but not the work of a man experienced in the difficult art of realising projects for the good of mankind." Now, it so happens that Ogilvie (who, by the way, was, for his day, a scientific agriculturist of the first rank, which Mackintosh was not) has incorporated in his text a "Scheme of a Progressive Agrarian Law" that speaks for itself. It embodies *the irreducible minimum of agrarian justice*, so to speak, and might, even at this hour, safely and without prejudice be submitted to the Collective Wisdom at St. Stephen's by the Salisbury Cabinet as " the basis of all partial and occasional reformation respecting property in land." Let the "gentlemen of England" weigh well its provisions, if they would avoid worse things—much worse—in the not remote future.

I. That every citizen, aged 21 years, may, if not already in possession of land, be entitled to claim from the public such extent of ground as may be cultivated to advantage by the ordinary family of a peasant—a husband, wife, and three children. This may be called the " standard farm," and ought to vary in extent according to the state of the country.

II. That the claimant shall have right to choose the situation of his allotment on any farm, freehold, or uncultivated common, if the same be not excepted by other provisions of this law.

III. This allotment shall be set apart, and its landmarks fixed by the magistrate, with the aid of arbitrators chosen by the parties.

IV. The arbitrators shall determine what reserved perpetual rent the claimant must pay to the landlord, and what temporary rent to the former tenant (if any) in compensation of their rights.

V. The following farms are to be exempted from such claims: (*a*) "Standard farms"; (*b*) lord of the manor's park or farm regulated by size of the estate; (*c*) farms not 10 years occupied by present tenant; (*d*) farms diminished one-half by this law exempted for 20 years to come; (*e*) farms of barren land taken for sake of improvement.

VI. In case the claimant is not contented with the rent affixed to his allotment, he shall not be obliged to hold it, but to pay the occupier twice the amount of any expense incurred by him. Every claimant may make four such options and no more.

VII. The person thus acquiring property shall continue to reside upon his farm. He shall have the right to transmit it to his heirs or assignees, but not to let it, or any part of it, on lease.

VIII. The father may choose to which of his sons the farm shall devolve, the lord of the manor being *ultimus hæres*.

IX. No allotment shall be united to another by succession.

X. It shall not be lawful to break down any such allotment in order to divide it among children, until in any county the uncultivated lands are wholly exhausted.

XI. The property in these allotments shall not carry along with it any right of common that is not founded on express contract.

XII. Those in possession of farms at the time of the enacting of this law shall not have any part thereof converted into freehold by its operation until by the option of other claimants these farms be reduced to an extent of less than 60 acres.

XIII. All who acquire property under this law shall be required to perform double militia service.

XIV. In every competition that may arise, orphans and those who have served in the army or navy shall be preferred to others.

XV. Every person who has acquired an allotment in this manner shall pay to the lord of the manor certain aids and services expedient for preserving order and subordination in the country without danger of giving rise to oppression or abuse.

In point of fact, Ogilvie, though a rigid logician and uncompromising theorist, recognised to the full that mankind are not governed by divine Reason but mostly by "that monster Custom which all sense doth eat of habit's devil," as Shakespeare hath it. He was, therefore, in practice, a "Possibilist" rather than either a visionary or a revolutionist. The object of his "Progressive Agrarian Law" was to get landlordism on an inclined plane, at the foot of which, once reached, it should remain innocuous for evermore. For he naïvely explains :—

"Without venturing to make openly any alteration in that system of landed property which, like systems of corrupted religion, is regarded with superstitious reverence in countries where it has long obtained, many occasions will occur whereof advantage may be taken to introduce under the cover of other objects, and as part of the usual proceedings of the State, such regulations (*e.g.*, Single Tax) very effectually, though by remote and indirect influence, *to promote the independence of the plough*, and the distribution of property in land among the lowest ranks of the people."

Above all things, the Prophet of Pittensear believed in the philosophy of "damnable iteration." "We must educate our new masters." Revolutions are advantageous, or the reverse, just in proportion as the people are prepared for them :—

" It is necessary that the object to be aimed at, and the means by which it may be obtained, should be again and again stated to the public in a variety of speculative views, and so rendered familiar to the understandings of men.

" Internal convulsions have arisen in many countries by which the decisive power of the State has been thrown, for a short while at least, into the hands of the Collective Body of the People. In these junctures they might have obtained a just re-establishment of their Natural Rights to Independence of Cultivation and to Property in Land HAD THEY BEEN THEMSELVES AWARE OF THEIR TITLE TO SUCH RIGHTS, and had there been any leaders prepared to direct them in the mode of stating their just claim, and supporting it with necessary firmness and becoming moderation. Such was the Revolution of 1688, at which time, surely, an article declarative of the Natural Right of Property in Land might have been inserted in the Bill of Rights, HAD THE PEOPLE AT LARGE BEEN BEFORE-HAND TAUGHT THAT THEY WERE POSSESSED OF ANY SUCH CLAIM. Such also was the late convulsion in

America (1776), the favourable opportunities of which are not yet exhausted." In 1899, alas, the people of the United States are nearly as landless as ourselves.

Adieu, wise, learned, and humane Prophet of Pittensear! May you sleep well!

Salve, nobilis Corona, Artium Parens, Patrona, Fortis Aberdoniæ!

THOMAS SPENCE

"THE MARTYR OF LAND LAW REFORM" (1775)

> "Not in vain Confessor old,
> Unto us the tale is told
> Of thy day of trial;
> Every age on him who strays
> From its broad and beaten ways
> Pours its sevenfold vial.
>
> "Thus with somewhat of the Seer
> Must the moral pioneer
> From the future borrow;
> Cloathe the waste with dreams of gain
> And on midnight's sky of rain
> Paint the golden morrow."—WHITTIER.

IT would be difficult even to conceive of two men more differently constituted by temperament and surroundings than William Ogilvie, "the Euclid of Land Law Reform," and his contemporary, Thomas Spence, the Martyr of the Cause.

All that birth and education could do for a man they had done for Ogilvie; for Spence they did nothing. And yet the same ideas laid hold of both thinkers with the force of irresistible conviction. This is briefly how it was with the self-taught plebeian.

Spence was born in 1750, in Newcastle-on-Tyne, one of a family of nineteen. His father was an Aberdonian, and his mother, Margaret Flet, an Orcadian. How many worthy citizens do we owe to the " Braif Toon," to be sure!

The elder Spence was a net-maker by trade, and his son, as a lad, acquired from him that humble art, and another infinitely more rare and difficult—the faculty of fearlessly thinking for himself on all manner of subjects. How this was achieved Spence himself tells us :—

" My father used to make my brothers and me read the Bible to him while working at his business ; and, at the end of every chapter, encouraged us to give our opinions on what we had just read. By these means I acquired an early habit of reflecting on every occurrence that passed before me, as well as on what I read."

Among the occurrences that shortly passed before Spence was one destined to change the whole current of his life and thought. The Corporation of Newcastle had seen fit to enclose a considerable section of the Town Moor or

Common, which they let in small farms or allotments. To the rents of these the Freemen of the borough laid claim as dividends. The Corporation (presumably a *co-opted* body) resisted, but was completely worsted in the law courts.

Enough! In the triumph of the Newcastle Freemen, Spence, by one sweeping induction, solved the entire Land Question. Let each parish periodically divide the rent of its soil among all the parishioners (due provision having first been made for public burdens), and the millennium would be no longer to seek. Eureka! Eureka!

At this juncture, Spence was twenty-five years of age, and no longer a net-maker, but a schoolmaster, and a member of the Philosophical Society of Newcastle-on-Tyne. He naturally hastened to communicate so notable a discovery to his brother philosophers. On November 8th, 1775, he read to them a wholly incontrovertible paper " On the Mode of Administering the Landed Estate of the Nation as a Joint Stock Property in Parochial Partnerships by Dividing the Rent." It was a complete solution of the land problem in a nutshell, so complete that I

defy any man, be he philosopher or fool, success-
fully to impugn it in any part.

The Newcastle philosophers did not attempt
refutation, but they made haste to expel him
from their precious society, and his school was
soon so effectively boycotted that he may be
said to have been expelled from Newcastle itself.
And the gravamen of Spence's offending was—
what do you suppose? Not the matter of the
essay, but the fact that Spence had it reprinted,
and "hawked about like a halfpenny ballad!"
To acquaint the common herd with their undeniable rights was an intolerable affront to all
well-regulated minds—a perfect outrage on divine
philosophy.

Now, what did this intrepid thinker really
propose? Without knowing it, perhaps, his aim
was to rehabilitate the primitive Commune (from
which, I believe, every departure has been a
disaster), and to adjust it to the conditions of
modern commercialism. "Spence's Plan" may
not be the final word on land tenure, but it will
admirably serve our Parish Councils to go on
with till a better is forthcoming. Here are the
essential points:—

" The land, *with all that appertains to it,* is, in every parish, made the property of the Corporation or parish, with as ample power to let, repair, or alter all or any part thereof, as a lord of the manor enjoys over his lands, houses, &c.; but the power of alienating the least morsel, in any manner, from the parish, either at this or any time hereafter, is denied. For it is solemnly agreed to, by the whole nation, that a parish that shall either sell or give away any part of its landed property shall be looked upon with as much horror and detestation as if they had sold all their children to be slaves, or massacred them with their own hands. Thus are there no more or other landlords in the whole country than the parishes, and each of them is sovereign lord of its territories.

" Then you may behold the rent which the people have paid into the parish treasuries employed by each parish in paying the Government its share of the sum which the Parliament or National Congress at any time grants; in maintaining and relieving its own poor people out of work; in paying the necessary officers their salaries; in building, repairing, and adorning its houses, bridges, and other structures; in making and maintaining convenient

and delightful streets, highways, and passages both
for foot and carriages; in making and maintaining
canals and other conveniences for trade and navigation; in planting and taking in waste grounds;
in providing and keeping up a magazine of am-
munition and all sorts of arms sufficient for all
the inhabitants in case of danger from enemies;
in premiums for the encouragement of agriculture, or anything else thought worthy of encouragement; and, in a word, doing *whatever the
people think proper*, and not, as formerly, to support and spread luxury, pride, and all manner
of vice.

" A man dwelling for a whole year in any parish
becomes a parishioner or member of its Corporation, and retains that privilege till he live a
full year in some other, when he becomes a member of that parish, and immediately loses all his
right to the former for ever, unless he chooses to
go back and recover it by dwelling again a full
year there. Thus none can be a member of two
parishes at once, and yet a man is always member
of one, though he move ever so oft.

" There are no taxes of any kind paid among
them, by native or foreigner, but the aforesaid

rent, which every person pays to the parish, according to the quantity, quality, and conveniences of the land, housing, &c., which he occupies in it. The Government, poor, roads, &c., are all maintained by the parishes with the rent, on which account all wares, manufactures, allowable trade employments, or actions are entirely duty free. Freedom to do anything whatever cannot there be bought; a thing is either entirely prohibited, as theft or murder, or entirely free to every one without tax or price; and the rents are still not so high, notwithstanding all that is done with them, as they were formerly, for only the maintenance of a few haughty, unthankful landlords.

" But though the rent, which includes all public burdens, were obliged to be somewhat raised, what then ? All nations have a devouring landed interest to support beside those necessary expenses of the public; and they might be raised very high indeed before their burden would be as heavy as that of their neighbours, who pay rent and taxes too.

" But what makes this prospect yet more glowing is, that after this empire of right and reason is thus established it will stand for ever. Force

and corruption attempting its downfall shall
equally be baffled, and all other nations, struck
with wonder and admiration at its happiness and
stability, shall follow the example; and thus the
whole earth shall at last be happy, and live like
brethren."

Spence's life was very chequered indeed, but it
does not appear, everything considered, to have
been an unhappy one. He lived for his ideas,
and they were meat and drink to him. Bewick,
the famous engraver, who knew him intimately,
describes him as " one of the warmest philan-
thropists of his day." Besides, he saw the comedy
as well as the tragedy of existence. Here is a
sample of his quaint humour. He calls it a
" Sylvan Joke," the incident occurring at Haydon
Bridge, about 1788 :—

" While I was in the wood alone by myself
a-gathering of nuts, the forester popped through
the bushes upon me, and, asking me what I did
there, I replied, ' Gathering nuts.'

" ' Gathering nuts !' said he, ' and dare you say
so ?'

" ' Yes,' said I, ' why not ? Would you question
a monkey or a squirrel about such a business ?

And am I to be treated as an inferior to one of these creatures, or have I a less right? But who are you,' continued I, 'that thus take it upon you to interrupt me?'

"'I'll let you know that,' said he, 'when I lay you.fast for trespassing here.'

"'Indeed,' answered I, 'but how can I trespass here where no man ever planted or cultivated; for these nuts are the spontaneous gift of Nature, ordained alike for the sustenance of man and beast that choose to gather them, and, therefore, they are common.'

"'I tell you,' said he, 'this wood is not common. It belongs to the Duke of Portland.'

"'Oh! My service to the Duke of Portland,' said I. 'Nature knows no more of him than of me. Therefore, as in Nature's storehouse, the rule is "first come first served," so the Duke of Portland must look sharp if he wants any nuts.'"

Spence, in conclusion, declared that if he were called upon to defend a country in which he durst not pluck a nut, he would throw down his musket, saying, "Let such as the Duke of Portland, who claim the country, fight for it!"

Eventually, like so many more ill-understood geniuses before and since, Spence found an asylum in London, where he opened a bookseller's shop at the corner of Chancery Lane, Holborn. Here, and afterwards at the " Hive of Liberty," Turnstile Street, Holborn, he published " Spence's Plan," " The Sun of Liberty," " Constitution of Spenconea, a Country in Fairyland," " Burke's Address to the Swinish Multitude " (in verse), " The End of Oppression," " The Rights of Infants, with Scriptures on Paine's ' Agrarian Justice,' " " Pigs' Meat ; or, Lessons for the Swinish Multitude," &c., &c.

" Pigs' Meat " (a weekly) was Spence's retort to Burke's scandalous phrase, the " Swinish Multitude." It is a well-selected series of reform readings from authors ancient and modern :—

" Collected (the old hero tells us) by the Poor Man's Advocate (that Veteran in the cause of Freedom), in the course of his reading for more than twenty years, and intended to promote among the labouring part of mankind proper ideas of their situation, of their importance, their rights ; and to convince them that their

forlorn condition has not been entirely overlooked and forgotten, nor their just cause un-
pleaded, neither by their Maker, nor by the best
and most enlightened men of all ages.

" Pigs' Meat " had appropriately for coat-of-
arms a superb pig, and for motto—

> " This is that matchless ' Pigs' Meat,'
> So famous far and near ;
> Oppressors' hearts it fills with dread,
> But poor men's hearts does cheer."

" Pigs' Meat " had an extensive sale, though
Spence caustically professed not to address it to
his own countrymen, but to savage races :—

" I beg, therefore, to be understood as laying
down a system of Government for the freeborn
unshackled minds of the North American and
African savages, who have not yet learned to
look upon Bloodsucking Landlords and State
Leeches with that timorous, superstitious, and
cringing reverence paid to such miscreants in a
country so well bred as this."

There is not a great deal more to be told of
Thomas Spence, the Martyr of Land Law Reform.
When Henry George wrote his " Progress and
Poverty," he knew nothing of the existence either

of Spence or of Ogilvie ; otherwise, I doubt not, his famous book would have been yet more famous and useful to mankind. It is a striking fault of English writers, accentuated as a rule in the case of American authors, that they are rarely well acquainted with what the Germans would call the " Encyclopædia" of their subject.

But even in this very ignorance there is a certain advantage. If they knew more of what eminent predecessors had done they would probably themselves, in many cases, feeling encumbered by the weight of their armour, do nothing at all. Spence felt himself a sort of Columbus of economic discovery, and, therefore, though fighting an almost single-handed battle against desperate odds, his determination to " spread the light," at all hazards, remained inflexible to the end. Except, perhaps, his predecessor, John Lilburne the Leveller, and his successor, Richard Carlile the Freethought Publisher, few, if any, Englishmen have ever been so despitefully entreated by the myrmidons of " Law and Order." He was constantly being tried, fined, imprisoned, and pillaged of his publications without seemingly any rhyme or reason.

Lord Kenyon and a special jury gave him twelve months in Shrewsbury Gaol for a series of perfectly reasonable, nay, most laudable, letters entitled " The Restorer of Society to its Natural State." " Seditious libel" they called it. They gave him no peace in prison or out of prison, and his domestic relations were unfortunately about as unhappy as his public.

He was twice married, and neither union was a success. Moral : *He who marries ideas should not marry wives.* Even Socrates found it so. Yet being asked by a disciple if it was well to marry, the sage replied : " Whether you do or not you will repent it," and that, peradventure, is the last word that can be said on the subject.

By his first wife, a Miss Elliot, he had one son, and he had to go to prison with his father, a circumstance which, needless to say, did not increase our land restorer's connubial felicity.

But Spence's second matrimonial venture was as disastrous as the courtship was, to say the least, unusual. One day, passing along a fashionable London Street, he noted an uncommonly handsome girl cleaning certain door steps. After observing her critically for a few moments,

Spence walked up to her and abruptly asked her if she would like to be married. Her reply was a decisive " Yes." " Well," said Spence, " name the day," and the day was there and then named, and a special licence obtained.

It turned out, however, that the girl had a sweetheart with whom she had just had a lovers' quarrel, and that her headlong rush into matrimony had but one object—to pique her lover. Spence treated her with the greatest kindness, but she took to evil ways, and eventually deserted him for a ship's captain, with whom she voyaged to the West Indies. Thence, after a time, she returned in misery to her husband, who again received her into his household, and did his utmost to make her happy. But she was a confirmed inebriate, and a separation was eventually effected, Spence making her the best weekly allowance he could out of his meagre income.

This curious episode in Spence's career has only one parallel coming within my personal cognisance, and, singularly enough, the result was (is) just the opposite. Some years ago, the brother of a very distinguished English baronet, one of the few baronets of my acquaintance, chanced to be travelling in the United States. (I took a letter of introduction to him from the worthy baronet when I was there.) He went into the splendid public library of Boston, and there saw a winsome and refined young Bostonian lady engaged in librarian duties. He chatted affably with her for a little, and then boldly asked her if she were fancy-free. She said, " Yes," and they made a compact there and then, " and lived happily ever afterwards."

In 1814 Spence started *The Giant Killer*, in Castle Street, Oxford Street ; but it had only reached its third number when he suddenly died in his sixty-fourth year. He had lived a most strenuous, useful, and disinterested life, and he was followed to the tomb by a numerous throng of devoted friends and admirers. Before the dead was carried to his resting-place in Tottenham Court graveyard, a pair of symbolic scales, each containing an equal quantity of earth, the balance being itself wreathed with white ribbon to denote the blameless character of the departed hero ; for hero he was in an infinitely truer sense than ever was Wolseley of

Coomassie, Roberts of Candahar, or Kitchener of Khartoum.

But Spence was destined to enjoy no rest even in his grave. Even in death he was deemed formidable by the "Classes." In 1817 the propaganda of the "Spenceans" led to the suspension of the Habeas Corpus˙ Act, when all the advocates of his "Plan," meeting in public, were made liable to transportation. The gallant Thistlewood and the "Cato Street Conspirators" were "Spenceans" to a man, though I doubt much if, under any circumstances, Spence himself could have been induced to take up arms for the realisation of his ideas. He saw the comedy of life too well to believe that force can ever be a real remedy for the wrongs he deplored.

This was one of his little conceits. To emphasise his "Plan" he had medals struck in copper. These it was his wont to jerk out of the window of his tenement in Holborn in great abundance, and hugely enjoy the scramble among the passers-by who mistook them for current coin of the realm.

One of these medals was inscribed, "Spence's Glorious Plan is Parochial Partnership without

Private Landlordism." On the reverse it was stated, " This Just Plan will produce everlasting Peace and Happiness—or, in fact, the Millennium."

Well, if the millennium is not here the fault is not to be laid at the door of dear old Thomas Spence, whose short way with landlords is immeasurably the shortest of any. He barely condescends to argue that all men's natural rights in the land are equal; and, indeed, the proposition is self-evident. What jurists are pleased to call " Acquired Rights" are merely *Force-established Wrongs*:—

" That property in land among men in a state of nature ought to be equal, few, one would be fain to hope, would be foolish enough to deny. Therefore, taking this to be granted, the country of any people, in a native state, is properly their *common*, in which each of them has an equal property with free liberty to sustain himself and family with the animals, fruits, and other products thereof. For upon what must they live if not upon the productions of the country in which they reside ? Surely to deny them that right is in effect denying them a right to live. The right to deprive anything of the means of living supposes a right to deprive it

of life.　Hence it is plain that the land, in any
country or neighbourhood, with everything in or
on the same, or pertaining thereto, belongs at all
times to the living inhabitants of the said country
or neighbourhood in an equal manner.　For there
is no living but on land and its productions; consequently, what we cannot live without we have the
same property in as our lives."

The above passage from the " Plan " may well
serve as a WHY for the subjoined WHEREFORE,
which, elsewhere in his writings, I once had the
good fortune to light upon in the British Museum.
I have oftener than once said that the words ought
to be blazoned in letters of gold wherever the
weary, toil-worn sons and daughters of the people
most do congregate.

" Let all the parishioners unite, take Archdeacon
Paley in the one hand and the Bible in the other,
assemble in the adjoining field, and, after having
discussed the subject to their own satisfaction,
enter into a Convention, and unanimously agree
to a Declaration of Rights, in which it is declared
that all the lands, including coal pits, mines, rivers,
&c., belonging to the Parish of Bees, now in the
possession of Lord Drone, shall, on Lady Day, 25th

March, 18—, become Public Property, the Joint-Stock and Common Farm, in which every parishioner shall enjoy an equal participation.

" *The same Declaration shall serve as a notice to Lord Drone to quit possession, and to give up all right and title to all the land, &c., he has hitherto possessed to the people of the said Parish of Bees on or before the above-mentioned day for ever.*

" And it may be further declared that, on Midsummer Day ensuing, all the rents arising from the lands, mines, rivers, coal-pits, &c., belonging to the said parish, instead of being paid as heretofore into the hands of Lord Drone or his Steward, shall be paid into the hands of a Parish Committee or Board of Directors, who may be appointed for that purpose, after being duly elected by a respectable majority of the whole parish; and that, after the National, Provincial, and Parochial Governments are provided for out of the rents thus collected, the remainder may be divided into equal shares among all the parishioners—men, women, and children—including Lord Drone and Lady Drone and all the little Drones belonging to the family, and the like division to be made on every succeeding quarter day for ever.

Well, if any man will undertake to dispose of Lord Drone and all the little Drones of the Drone family, in briefer or more intelligible terms than the above, all I can say is, he deserves a statue in Westminster Abbey a thousand times more than nine-tenths of those that figure, or rather *disfigure*, in that choicest collection of first-class scoundrels to be found anywhere in Christendom.

But, though Spence himself has, naturally enough, no statue, his memory has not perished. The *English Land Restoration League,* and indeed all Collectivists, are " Spenceans," with this shade or that of differentiation.

Mr. Fred. Verinder, the ever-vigilant secretary of the *E.L.R.L.*, has thus clearly discriminated between the older "Spenceans" and their "Modern" congeners :—

"The 'object' of the League is stated, as frankly as Spence himself could have wished, to be 'the abolition of landlordism.' As to method, 'Don't *kick* the landlords out, don't *buy* them out, but TAX them out,' says the League. Spence's unceremonious 'notice to quit' to Lord Drone finds its echo in the League's constant protest against compensation or land purchase in any shape or form. 'Spence's Plan' and the League's plan are two ways of stating the same proposals. 'There are no taxes of any kind . . . but the aforesaid rent,' says the former. 'The abolition of all taxation upon labour and the products of labour and the earnings of labour, and the imposition of a tax of 20s. in the pound on the value of all land,' is the programme of the latter. And on no point in Spence's plan does the League more strongly insist, than upon his protest against the alienation into private hands of any portion of the land which is now, or hereafter may become, public property. A comparison of the publications of the League with the writings of the Newcastle Schoolmaster will make it abundantly clear that the Land Restorers of to-day are fairly entitled to the honour of being called the 'Modern Spenceans.' "

Allen Davenport, a warm friend and admirer of the Martyr of Land Law Reform, wrote his epitaph in lines which, I fear, are not poetry. Indeed, they are doggerel; but, unlike much poetry and most epitaphs, they have the superlative merit of being true to life and letter :—

> " All Nature's laws he freely, clearly scanned,
> And found the *summum bonum* in the Land ;

And showed that Justice planted in the Earth
Gave man new Rights and Liberty new birth :
And formed a plan on the Agrarian Scheme
Which we, grown wise, know to be no dream.
That man, that honest man, was Thomas Spence,
Whose genius, judgment, wit, and manly sense
Confounded all the dogmas of the schools,
And proved that Statesmen are but learned fools :
That Priests preach future worlds of pain and bliss
To cheat the weak and rob the poor in this ;
Or else their practice and their cry would be,
' Let all be Equal and let all be Free ! ' "

THOMAS PAINE

"THE POLITICIAN OF LAND LAW REFORM"

(1796)

> " Thy logic vanquished error, and thy mind
> No bounds but those right and truth confined.
> Thy soul of fire must e'en ascend the sky—
> Immortal Paine, thy fame can never die ;
> For men like thee their names must ever save
> From the black edicts of the tyrant grave.
>
> As Euclid clear his various writings shone ;
> His pen, inspired by glorious truth alone,
> O'er all the earth diffusing light and life,
> Subduing error, ignorance, and strife ;
> To this immortal man, to Paine, 'twas given
> To metamorphose earth from hell to heaven."
>
> —CLIO RICKMAN.

OF Jerrard Winstanley the "Digger," William Ogilvie the "Euclid," and Thomas Spence the "Martyr" of the land problem, I have been at pains to record all, or nearly all, the meagre personal memorabilia it is now possible to discover; but of Thomas Paine's world-renowned career, except in so far as he was a precursor of Henry George as a Land Law Reformer, I need here only speak in very general terms.

Years ago I wrote a short "Life of Thomas Paine, Rationalist and Revolutionist," but that and every other tribute to the immortal memory of the author of the "Rights of Man" and the "Age of Reason" have since then been completely superseded by my friend Dr. Moncure D. Conway's monumental edition of "Paine's Life and Works."

The character of Carlyle's "rebellious needleman" has been so completely vindicated that, thank God, it can never more be blasted by the rank breath of political calumny or religious hate. He has taken his place irrevocably among "Plutarch's Men."

Born at Thetford, Norfolk, 1737, of poor Quaker parents, "Tom" was from his very childhood an original thinker. His mind was so constituted that it could accept nothing on mere authority or trust. His inflexible intellectual honesty was as marked as that of Lucian, Bruno, Servetus, Voltaire, or Hume.

Paine's schooling was of a meagre kind, not extending beyond "the three R.'s." But it may be safely affirmed that, if the individuality had been crushed out of him by a collegiate education, he would never have bestowed on the world the most splendid political treatise ever penned, "The Rights of Man."

In 1774 he sailed for America, armed with a letter of introduction from Benjamin Franklin. In England he had put his hand to a variety of occupations, trying in vain to find some true sphere of action in life. He had learned stay-making with his father—hence Carlyle's "rebellious needleman"; had served on board a man-of-war; had been an exciseman; had been a grocer, and sold tobacco; had been a schoolmaster in Kensington. But, in whatever circumstances he found himself, Paine's pursuit of useful (never useless) knowledge was unflagging. "Indeed," said he, "I have seldom passed five minutes of my life, however circumstanced, in which I did not acquire some knowledge."

Strange to say, he was indifferent to affairs of State. His natural bent was towards science, and he became an adept in mathematical, mechanical, and astronomical studies. In 1788 he erected a great iron bridge at Rotherham, in Yorkshire, on a principle of construction which has stood the tests of science and of time. "But," says Paine, "I had no disposition for what was called politics.

It presented to my mind no other idea than is
contained in the word *jockeyship.*"

In revolutionary America Paine at once found
scope for his latent genius, defined by Plato as
" wisdom drinking at the fountain of enthusiasm."
His famous "Common Sense," thrown like the
sword of Brennus into the scale against con-
ciliation with Britain's Mad Monarch and his
detestable ministers, rendered the ever memorable
" Declaration of Independence" inevitable.   Paine
was the first man who ever wrote the fateful
words : " *The Free and Independent States of
America.*"   At the close of the war, it is not too
much to say that Paine stood on as lofty a
pedestal of popular esteem as Washington, Jefferson, Franklin, or Adams.

But to rest was foreign to his nature.   His
maxim was, " Where Freedom is *not,* there is my
country."   In 1788 he sailed for France, which
had caught the revolutionary infection from
America.   In 1791–92 his "Rights of Man" appeared in London, and never did the Society of
Privilege and Make - believe receive a blow so
staggering.   The author was, of course, duly in-
dicted and convicted, but before judgment could

be given Paine was a member of the French Convention, and beyond the jurisdiction of the Court.

All through the agony of the French Revolution Paine's conduct was marked by English moderation and good sense, qualities which, in the awful days of the Terror, brought him within an ace of the guillotine. Indeed, he escaped by nothing short of a miracle.

On his return to the United States his reception was anything but what it ought to have been. For why? After looking into the pretensions of kings, he had thought well, in his prison-cell in the Luxembourg, with the knife of the guillotine hourly glistening before his eyes, to investigate those of the priests. They never forgave him, and, although the conclusions at which he arrived in the "Age of Reason" are practically indistinguishable from those of most Unitarians, many Quakers, and much of the "higher criticism" of the hour, it is still a tenet of orthodox belief that he was a "blaspheming Infidel and Atheist."

He was, in point of fact, a convinced Theist, a preacher at times to a Theistic congregation, a believer in the immortality of the soul, and a respecter of the Christ of the Evangelist as "A Prophet mighty in deed and word before God and all the People." And he died as he lived, one of the grandest exemplars of intellectual piety, fidelity, and rectitude that ever breathed.

But in my enthusiasm for the good name of sorely-maligned Thomas Paine, I am forgetting that my real business with him for the present is as a precursor of Henry George, the character in which he is least of all known in our day. How few even of enlightened Socialist readers are aware that the author of "The Rights of Man" is also the author of "Old-Age Pensions," and something more. How few have ever perused Paine's

AGRARIAN JUSTICE

OPPOSED TO

AGRARIAN LAW

AND

AGRARIAN MONOPOLY;

BEING A PLAN FOR

Meliorating the Condition of Men

By Creating in every Nation

A NATIONAL FUND,

To pay to every Person, when arrived at the Age of Twenty-one Years, the Sum of Fifteen Pounds Stg., to enable Him or Her to begin the World.

Ten Pounds* per Annum during Life to
every Person now Living, of the Age of
Fifty Years, and to All Others when they
shall arrive at that Age, to enable them
to live in Old Age without Wretchedness,
and to go decently out of the World.

It is noteworthy that in theory Paine was almost,
if not altogether, at one with his contemporaries,
Spence and Ogilvie, on the Land Question. Here
is his ground :—

"It is a position not to be controverted that the
earth, in its natural, uncultivated state, was, and
ever would have continued to be, the common
property of the human race. In that state every
man would have been born to property. He would
have been a joint life-proprietor with the rest in
the property of the soil, and in all its natural productions, vegetable and animal. But the earth, in
its natural state, is capable of supporting but a
small number of inhabitants compared with what
it is capable of doing in a cultivated state. And
as it is impossible to separate the improvement
made by cultivation from the earth itself upon
which that improvement is made, the idea of
landed property arose from that inseparable con-

* Then a "living wage.

nection; but it is nevertheless true that it is the value of the improvement only, and not the earth itself, that is individual property. Every proprietor, therefore, of cultivated land owes to the community a *ground-rent*, for I know no better term to express the idea by, for the land which he holds; and it is from this ground-rent that the fund proposed in this plan is to issue."

Paine, as will be seen, speaks only of appropriating the ground-rent of "cultivated land," the monstrous yield of urban house-sites being then in its infancy. But what is true of the one is even truer of the other, inasmuch as the plunder of the community is more glaring and indefensible in the case of the proprietor of building sites. Paine continues : —

" Cultivation is, at least, one of the greatest improvements ever made by human invention. It has given to created earth a tenfold value ; but the Land Monopoly, that began with it, has produced the greatest evil. It has dispossessed more than half the inhabitants of every nation of their natural inheritance, without providing for them, as ought to have been done, an indemnification for their loss ; and has thereby created a species of poverty and wretchedness that did not exist. In advocating the case of the persons thus dispossessed it is a right, and not a charity, I am pleading for."

How this right is to be enforced, and a national compensation fund is to be created, Paine then proceeds to show in conclusive details with which every student of the old-age problem ought to acquaint himself, though they are a trifle too dry and *actuarial* for the general reader. France, for which the scheme was proposed, had at the time (1796) to meet all the heavy monetary exigencies of the Revolution, and fresh taxation of the ordinary type was out of the question. Let us, therefore, argued Paine, adopt—

" A method (Death Duties) the least troublesome and the most effectual, and also because the subtraction will be made at a time that best admits it, which is, at the moment that property is passing by the death of one person to the possession of another. In this case the bequeather gives nothing. The only matter to him is that the monopoly of natural inheritance, to which there never was a right, begins to cease in his person. A generous man would wish it not to continue, and a just man will rejoice to see it abolished. I have no property in France to become subject to the plan I propose. What I have, which is not much, is in the United States of America. But I will pay £100 towards this fund in France the instant it shall be established, and I will pay the same sum in England whenever a similar establishment shall take place in that country."

In the Preface to "Agrarian Justice," Paine thus comments on a sermon by Watson, Bishop of Llandaff, entitled "The Wisdom and Goodness of God in having made both Rich and Poor," and with his striking words I conclude :—

"The error contained in the title of this sermon determined me to publish my 'Agrarian Justice.' It is wrong to say God made rich and poor; He made only male and female, and gave them the earth for their inheritance. Instead of preaching to encourage one part of mankind in insolence, it would be better that the priests employed their time in rendering the condition of men less miserable than it is. Practical religion consists in doing good; and the only way of serving God is that of endeavouring to make His Creation happy. All preaching that has not this for its object is nonsense and hypocrisy."

Yea, verily !

PATRICK EDWARD DOVE

"THE SCIENTIST OF LAND LAW REFORM"

(1850)

" Inequality is the source of all revolutions, for no compensation can make up for inequality."—*Aristotle.*

" The earth belongs in usufruct to the living. The dead have no rights over those who now exist."—*Thomas Jefferson.*

" The greatest of all injustice is that which goes under the name of *law;* and of all sorts of tyranny the forcing of the letter of the law against *equity* is the most insupportable."—*L'Estrange.*

"The Lord shall enter into judgment with the ancients of His people, and the princes thereof : for ye have eaten up the vineyards ; the spoil of the poor is in your houses. And what mean ye that ye beat My people to pieces, and grind the faces of the poor ? "—*Isaiah.*

I NOW come to speak of Patrick Edward Dove, the fourth of the five great precursors of Henry George. If Jerrard Winstanley the " Digger " was the " Seer " of the Land Question, Thomas Spence its " Martyr," William Ogilvie its " Euclid," and Thomas Paine its " Politician," Patrick Edward Dove may well be termed its " Scientist."

Dove was born in the year of Waterloo, on 31st July (my own natal day), at Lasswade,

near Edinburgh.   His father, Lieutenant Henry
Dove, R.N., was an Englishman of good family,
originally of Surrey stock, but settled in Devon-
shire since 1716.

For generations the Doves had been officers in
the Royal Navy, and it was Patrick's earnest wish
to follow in the ancestral footsteps; but his father
luckily had other views for his son's future.   The
Napoleonic wars were over, and the elder Dove
wisely determined that his promising lad should
cultivate the arts of peace.

The youth's education—chiefly acquired in
England and France—was rather desultory, and
terminated somewhat abruptly.   Having headed a
schoolboy riot, of the not unusual anti-dominie
order, he was expelled the seminary, and in 1830
his father packed him off to Scotland to learn
scientific farming.

Thence he found his way successively to Paris,
Spain, and London, developing the while a physical,
intellectual, and moral nature of the manliest
type.

In 1841 he acquired the estate of Craig, near
Ballantrae, Ayrshire, a locality familiar to every
reader of Louis Stevenson's "Master of Ballantrae."

As horseman, shot, fly-fisher, sailor, mechanic, gun-maker, his pre-eminence was unchallenged. He would have no gamekeeper about him, because he was wholly opposed to the Game Laws. He acted as adviser-general to all the farmers of the neighbourhood, and when the potato famine occurred in 1846, he exerted himself with characteristic energy to mitigate the suffering of the peasantry by devising means of employment.

In 1848 his career as a country gentleman came to an end through the loss of most of his fortune in an unlucky speculation. But it mattered little to Dove, who never worshipped at the shrine of Mammon. He set out for Darmstadt to study German philosophy, and while still there, there appeared (1850) in London Part I. of his great work, "The Elements of Political Science, otherwise the Theory of Human Progression and Natural Probability of a Reign of Justice." The volume made the deepest impression on the most discerning, Sir William Hamilton and Thomas Carlyle in this country being among its warmest applauders. In America the celebrated Jurist and Senator, Charles Sumner, had it stereotyped, and at his request Dove in 1853 wrote a powerful

article on slavery, in the *Boston Commonwealth*,
entitled "The Elder and Younger Brother."

Dove now settled in Edinburgh, and there lectured, in the Philosophical Institution, on "Heroes
of the Commonwealth" (1853), "Wild Sports of
Scotland" (1854), "The Crusades" (1855). He
excelled as a lecturer as in everything to which
he applied his redundant energies. In 1854 he
edited for six months, during the illness of his
friend, Hugh Miller, of geologic and other fame,
the *Witness* newspaper, and in that year moreover
was published at Edinburgh Part II. of "The Elements of Social Science," from which are taken most
of the subjoined excerpts on the Land Question.

In 1855 appeared "Romanism, Rationalism, and
Protestantism," a vigorous vindication of the last-
named "ism." In 1856 Dove essayed to succeed
the renowned Sir William Hamilton in the Chair
of Metaphysics in Edinburgh University. Carlyle,
among others, backed him for all he was worth;
but the post, unfortunately, went to another, who
failed not, however, loyally to testify to his com-
petitor's "powerful individuality in a union of
fervid practical aim, with uncommon speculative
grasp and insight." Dove was *Scotis ipsis Scottior*.

In Dove's case the adage, "jack of all trades and master of none," was strikingly falsified. He was master of all. He published a notable treatise on the "Revolver," and invented or perfected a rifled cannon of great range and precision. He was an enthusiastic volunteer, and in 1859 he was appointed to the command of the 91st Lanarkshire Rifles. At the first meeting of the National Rifle Association at Wimbledon he won several prizes.

But his literary and scientific activity never flagged. In 1858 he went to Glasgow to edit the *Commonwealth,* superintending at the same time the publication of "The Imperial Dictionary of Biography." He, moreover, edited, in conjunction with Professor Macquorn Rankine, "The Imperial Journal of the Arts and Sciences," and the masterly article "Government" in the *Encyclopædia Britannica* was contributed by him.

In 1860 this Admirable Crichton, like so many more seemingly tireless brain-workers, was visited by a stroke of paralysis, which irremediably shattered the delicate organism of his noble intellect. In vain hope of recovery he went to Natal in 1862, returned in 1863, and died of gradual "softening of the brain" in 1873.

It is one of the regrets of my life that I never
even saw Patrick Edward Dove in the flesh; but
I have been told by those who knew him well that
his presence and personality were of the noblest,
and I can well believe it, if the whole-souled
thoroughness of his "Elements of Social Science"
is to be taken as any criterion. Dear old Professor John Stuart Blackie, among other friends,
often spoke of Dove, and his witness was this:—

"Dove combined, in a remarkable degree, the
manly directness of the man of action with the
fine speculation of the man of thought. Altogether
he dwells in my mind as one of the most perfect
types of the manly thinker whom I have met in a
long life."

But now let us turn from the *res gestæ* of the
illustrious thinker to a few of his masculine
thoughts on the all-important Land Question:—

"How Rent Originates.

"Rents, then, originate in this manner: Accórd-
ing to the constitution of the terrestrial world, as
framed by God in its suitability to man's requirements, earth produces *more* than the cost of the
labour requisite to obtain the productions. This

more is the surplus produce which remains in excess over and above what man requires to consume while engaged in labouring. This surplus is the *natural profit of labour*, and it represents the extra-productive capacity of the soil—that is, the capacity of the soil to furnish more produce than the labour required to consume. The surplus produce is the measure of the extra capacity, and it is this extra capacity (which represents the *natural profit of labour*) for which rent is payable. . . .

" Let us, then, clearly understand that rent originates in the fact that the earth is (or has become) capable of returning for one man's labour not only as much as will support one man, but as much as will support two or three, or more men; so that the man who labours on the earth receives not only the cost of his labour, but a profit equal to the cost, or *double* the cost. And rent is the price paid for the capacity of producing this profit. But, in saying that the cultivator receives this *profit*, it is of course to be understood that it is not profit to *him* unless it remains in his hands."

" PRIVATE RENT IS HISTORICALLY MISAPPROPRIATED PUBLIC TAXATION.

" The rent of any one portion of soil does *not* depend on the labour or capital that has been expended on that portion. For instance, if, in the heart of London, a space of twenty acres had been enclosed by a high wall at the time of the Norman Conquest, and if no man had ever touched that portion of soil, or even seen it from that time to this, it would, if let by auction, produce an enormously high rent. . . . It is a well-known and commonly observed fact, that the establishment of manufactures greatly increases the rent of the surrounding soil—in fact, that this increase of rent has been *created* by the manufacturers. But a fact of much greater importance, and one not commonly made the matter of distinct reflection is this, *that manufacturers create all the legitimate rent that can possibly exist,* all other payment being in reality either *taxation* or *robbery.* And thus the present rents of the landholders are really and truly *transformed taxation*—that is, the amount now paid to the landlord in the shape of rent is the modern representative of what was formerly paid to the State in the shape of taxation, the tax for the State service being transformed into the rents of the individual landlords. And thus the labouring classes, who formerly paid only taxation, now pay both rent *and* taxation, and consequently are *robbed,* for *robbery* it is (see Whately's Logic), of the *profits* of their labours. With a purely agricultural population there can be no *rent*—there may be *taxation,* that is, *payment out of the profits of labour for the service of the State,* or there may be *robbery,* that is, *payment extracted by force out of the profits of labour to support a non-labouring aristocracy.* And as human Society, in its present form, grew gradually out of the feudal constitution of Society in which the aristocrat was the State-soldier, the lands which were the *benefices* of the State-soldier were transformed into the property of the individual, independent, and non-responsible landlord—a few thousands of whom now enjoy what was formerly the *taxation* of the kingdom, while the labourers have to pay *another taxation* equal to the rents of the soil."

"Logic of the Single Tax.

"To whom, then, *ought* the rents of the soil to be equitably allocated?

"I do not hesitate to say to the Nation. For the service of the nation, taxes must be derived from some quarter or other; and if the taxes had always been derived from the rents of the soil, there never would have been any tax on industry, any Custom House, any Excise, or any of those restrictive measures that repress industry, while they eminently contribute to separate nation from nation, and to prevent the commercial intercourse that ultimately would have abolished war. National Property there must be *somewhere*, and assuredly it is more *just* to take that property from the natural value of the soil than from the individual fruits of labour. From one or other it *is* and *must* be taken; and if there would be injustice in taking it from the impersonal rent of the soil, there is certainly more injustice in taking it from the profits of individual exertion."

" Specific Advantages of the Single Tax.

" Several special advantages would attend the allocation of the rents of the soil to the nation.

" *First.*—All Customs and Excise might be abolished. This would permit a perfectly free trade with all countries, and a perfectly free trade would tend to unite the various nations in a bond of amity. It would also set free for useful industry a great army of unproductive workers.

" *Second.*—It would make one simple tax, which could be collected without expense.

" *Third.*—It would unite the agricultural and manufacturing classes into one common interest. The greater the revenue, the *better* it would be for the nation; whereas now, the greater the revenue, the worse for the nation.

" *Fourth.*—It would secure the utmost possible production that the soil was capable of affording.

" *Fifth.*—It would eminently tend to secure the education of the people, because—as the State would be directly interested in the labours of every man, and an educated population would always be more productive than an ignorant

population — the State might consequently be
trusted to suppress all that was detrimental to
their welfare; to encourage skill, industry, and
talent by providing the fullest possible instruction for the whole nation; for the more the
people were educated the more intelligent would
all labour become, and the more would the
national revenue increase under the influence of
intelligent labour.

" *Sixth.*—It would secure to every labourer his
share of the previous labours of the community.
It is quite evident that a greater amount of
outlay has been made on the island of Great
Britain than on any other part of the world of
similar extent.   Yet the labourer who inherits all
these facilities is not so well off as in Arkansas
or Wisconsin, where no capital has been pre-
viously expended.   This in itself is a sufficient
proof that there is something wrong in the very
construction of Society; for, undoubtedly, a man
born in a country where thousands of millions
have been expended in rendering that country
more suitable for man's requirements ought to
find his labour better remunerated than in a
country that remains in a state of nature.

" *Seventh.*—The allocation of the rents of the soil to the nation is the only possible means by which a *just* distribution of the created wealth can be effected. It is true, this is not the only requisite —*for* (*N.B.* Socialists !) *a systematic co-operation in the whole field of labour is also needful*—but the first main requisite, the first necessary arrangement of society which would prevent the profits of labour from escaping, as they now continually do, *from* the labourers *to* a class that labours *not,* yet constantly increases its wealth ! "

"Landlords are the Natural Enemies of God and Man.

" It is the law of God, as declared in the constitution of the terrestrial world, and the law of Christianity, as declared in the written Scriptures, that the industrious man should be rich; and that the man who labours not should be poor. The whole economy of Britain is a direct infringement of this great law of property—of this great and fundamental principle which God established for the economical government of the world, when He made the earth to yield its riches in return

for human labour. The richest men in England
are those who do *not* labour, and who never did
labour. And their wealth is secured in such a
manner that it descends from generation to generation, and goes on constantly increasing without
any exertion on their part. Were they to sleep
for a hundred years, they would wake more
wealthy than ever; and if they did wake, they
would wake only to encumber the industry of
the country, to retard its progress, to prevent the
amendment of its institutions, and to maintain a
party warfare against its real prosperity. As a
class, they are antagonistic to industry, enemies
to freedom and to progress, barriers to the civilisation of the world, living on the fruits of other
men's labours, yet hating and despising the toil
which alone endows them with wealth."

"GLIMPSE OF THE PROMISED LAND.

"This is the true, and the only true, theory of a
NATION—that the soil belongs to it in perpetuity,
and never can be alienated from it; and that he
who will give the greatest rent for the soil becomes its cultivator, and pays the rent to the

nation for the benefit of the whole community. Then, but not till then, will labour reap its natural reward—the reward appointed by Providence in the divine constitution of the terrestrial economy. Then will the welfare of one be the welfare of all; then will men be banded together by a true citizenship; and then will the first great step be taken towards that mighty Brotherhood which springs from our common parentage, and which is at once the promise and the prophecy of the Christian faith—

> 'And man to man the warld ower
> Shall brothers be an a' that.'"

Vale! Greatheart Dove! Of thee Nature might well stand up and say to all the world, "This *was* a Man!"

JERRARD WINSTANLEY

"*THE DIGGER*" (1649)

" I have also seen wisdom under the sun on this wise, and it seemed great unto me.

" There was a little city and few men within it ; and there came a great king against it and besieged it, and built great bulwarks against it.

" Now there was found in it a poor wise man, and he by his wisdom delivered the city ; yet no one remembered that same poor man.

" Then said I, Wisdom is better than Strength ; nevertheless the poor man's wisdom is despised, and his words are not heard.

" Wisdom is better than weapons of war ; but one sinner devoureth much good."—*Ecclesiastes* ix. 13, 14, 15, 16, 18.

A GOOD man $\mathsf{\mathbf{y}}$ years have now elapsed since I made a more or less successful effort to rescue from oblivion the memory of Lieutenant-Colonel John Lilburne, the Leveller—"Free-born John" the Cavaliers called him—the *man of action* of the Socialistic party in the English Commonwealth. Lilburne was every inch a hero, "the most turbulent, but the most upright and courageous of mankind," according to Historian Hume. He was the author of the famous "Agreement of the

People," the "People's Charter" in its earliest form—the very foundation-stone of modern democracy in Europe and America.

Then, also, I caught my first distinct glimpse of the great *thinker* of the Levellers, Jerrard Winstanley the "Digger," on this wise, in Bulstrode - Whitelocke's invaluable contemporary, "Memorials of English Affairs." He notes, under date 17th April 1649, that "the General (Fairfax) sent two troops of horse to have account of certain Levellers at St. Margaret's Hill, near Cobham, and St. George's Hill, inasmuch as they digged the ground and sowed it with roots and beans," and, on 20th April, there is the following instructive entry in the diary:—

"Everard and Winstanley, the chief of those that digged at St. George's Hill, in Surrey, came to the General and made a Large Declaration to justify their proceedings—

"'That all the Liberties of the People were lost by the coming of William the Conqueror, and that ever since the People of God had lived under tyranny and oppression worse than that under the Egyptians.

"'But God would bring His People out of the

slavery, and restore them to their freedom in enjoying the fruits and benefits of the earth.

"'That they intend not to meddle with any man's property nor to break down any enclosures, only to meddle with what was common and untilled to make it fruitful for the use of man, and that the time will be that all men shall willingly come in and give up their lands and estates and submit to the Community.

"'And for those who should come and work they should have meat, drink, and clothes, which is all that is necessary to the life of man, and that for *money* there was no need of it, nor of clothes more than to cover nakedness.

"'That they will not defend themselves by arms, but will submit to authority and wait till the promised opportunity be offered, which they conceive to be at hand.'

"While they were before the General they stood with their hats on, and being demanded the reason thereof they said he was but their fellow-creature."

This "Large Declaration" Winstanley promptly followed up with a vigorous "Letter to the Lord Fairfax and his Council of War, with divers

Questions to Lawyers and Ministers: Proving it an undeniable Equity, That the Common People ought to dig, plough, plant, and dwell upon the Commons (lands) without hiring them or paying Rent to any."

In said "Letter" Fairfax is thus admonished:—

"We told you upon a question you put to us (when you were at our works upon the Hill) that we were not against any that would have Magistrates and Laws to govern, as the nations of the world are governed; but as for our parts, we should need neither the one nor the other, for as our land is common, so our cattle is to be common, and are not to be bought and sold amongst us, but to remain a standing portion of livelihood to us, and our children, without the cheating entanglement of Buying and Selling.

"What need, then, have we of any outward, selfish, confused laws, made to uphold the power of covetousness, when we have the Righteous Law written in our hearts, teaching us to walk purely in the creation?"

Then come the following pertinent posers for his Lordship and his Worshipful Council's advisers learned in the law:—

" We desire that your lawyers may consider these questions, which we affirm to be truths:

" 1. Whether William the Conqueror came not to be King of England by Conquest; turned the English out of their birthrights; and compelled them for necessity of livelihood to be servants to him and his Norman soldiers?

" 2. Whether King Charles (I.) was not successor to the Crown of England from William the Conqueror? And whether all laws that have been made in every king's reign did not confirm and strengthen the power of the Norman Conquest; and so did, *and do still,* hold the Commons of England under slavery to the kingly power, his gentry, and clergy?

" 3. Whether Lords of Manors were not the successors of the colonels and chief officers of William the Conqueror, and held their royalty over the common (lands) by lease, grant, and patents from the King; and *the power of the sword* was and is their only title?

" 4. Whether Lords of Manors have not lost their royalty to the common land since the Common People of England, as well as some of the gentry, have conquered King Charles, and recovered themselves from under the Norman Conquest ?

" 5. Whether the Norman Conqueror took the land of England to himself out of the hands of a few men, called a Parliament, or from the whole body of the English People ? Surely he took freedom from every one; and what benefit shall the Common People have that have suffered most in these wars by the victory that is got over the King ? It had been better for the Common People there had been no such victory, for they are impoverished in their estates by free quarters and taxes, and made worse to live than they were before.

" 6. Whether the freedom, which the Common People have got by casting out the kingly power, lie not here principally : To have the land of their nativity for their livelihood freed from the entanglement of lords, lords of manors, and landlords, who are our taskmasters ? Seeing all sorts of people have given assistance to recover England from under the Norman yoke, surely all sorts ought to have their freedom, not compelling one to work for wages for another.

" 7. Whether any laws, since the coming in of kings, have been made in the light of the righteous

Law of our Creation, respecting all alike; or have not been grounded upon selfish principles, in fear or flattery of their king, to uphold freedom in the gentry and clergy, and to hold the Common People under bondage?

" 8. Whether all Laws that are not grounded on Equity and Reason, not giving a universal freedom to all, but respecting persons, *ought not to be cut off with the King's head?* We affirm they ought. If all Laws be grounded on Equity and Reason, then the whole Land of England is to be a common treasury to every one that is born in the Land; but, if they be grounded on selfish principles (giving freedom to some and laying burdens upon others), such Laws *are to be cut off with the King's head;* or else the neglectors are covenant, oath, and promise-breakers, and open hypocrites to the world.

" 9. Whether every one, without exception, ought not to have liberty to enjoy the Earth for his livelihood, and to settle his dwelling in any part of the Commons of England, without buying or renting land of any; seeing every one, by agreement and covenant among themselves, have paid taxes, given free quarter, and adventured their lives to recover England out of bondage? We affirm they ought.

"10. Whether the Laws that were made in the days of the Kings do give freedom to any other people but the gentry and clergy? All the rest are left servants and bondsmen to those task-masters. Surely, if the Common People have no more freedom in England but only to live among their elder brothers, and work for them for hire; what freedom, then, have they in England more than we can have in Turkey or France? For *there*, if any man will work for wages, he may live among them; otherwise not."

Then come the following conundrums to "Public Preachers that *say* they preach the Righteous Law":—

"*First*, We demand, Yea or Nay, whether the Earth, with her fruits, was made to be bought and sold from one to another? And whether one part of mankind was made a lord of the land, and another part a servant, by the Law of Creation before the Fall.

"I affirm (and challenge you to disprove) that the Earth was made to be a Common Treasury of livelihood for all, without respect of persons,

and was not made to be bought and sold: and
that mankind, in all his branches, is lord over
the beasts, birds, fishes, and the Earth; and was
not made to acknowledge any of his own kind
to be his Teacher and Ruler, but the Spirit of
Righteousness only his maker, and to walk in
His light and so to live in peace. And this being
a truth, as it is, then none ought to be lords or
landlords over another, but the Earth is free for
every son or daughter of mankind to live free
upon.

"This question is not to be answered by any
text of Scripture, or example since the Fall;
but the answer is to be given *in the light of
itself*, which is the Law of Righteousness; or
that word of God which was in the beginning,
which dwells in man's heart, and by which he
was made; even the pure law of Creation, unto
which the Creation is to be restored.

" Before the Fall, Adam (or the Man) did
dress the garden (or the Earth) in love, freedom, and righteousness, which was his rest and
peace; but when covetousness began to rise up
in him to kill the power of love and freedom in
him, and so made him (mankind) to set himself

one man above another, as Cain lifted up himself above Abel; which was but the outward
declaration of the two powers that strive in
Adam's (Man's) heart: and when he consented
to that Serpent (Covetousness), then he fell
from righteousness, was cursed, and sent into
the Earth to eat his bread in sorrow. And from
that time began particular propriety to grow
in one man over another; and the sword brought
in propriety, and holds it up, which is no other
but the power of angry Covetousness; for Cain
killed Abel, because Abel's principles (or religion) were contrary to his. And the Power
of the Sword is still Cain killing Abel, lifting up
one man still above another. But Abel shall
not always be slain, nor always lie under the
bondage of Cain's cursed propriety, for he must
rise. And that Abel of old was but a type of
Christ, that is now rising up to restore all things
from bondage.

"*Secondly*, I demand, Whether all wars, bloodshed, and misery came not upon the Creation,
when one man endeavoured to be a lord over
another? Your Scripture will prove this sufficiently to be true. And whether this misery

shall not remove (and not till then), when all
the branches of mankind shall look upon themselves as One Man, and upon the Earth as a
Common Treasury to all, without respecting
persons; every one acknowledging the Law of
Righteousness in them and over them, and
walking in His light purely? Then cast away
your Buying and Selling the Earth with her
fruits. It is unrighteous, it lifts one above
another, it makes one man oppress another,
and is the burthen of Creation.

" *Thirdly*, Whether the work of restoration
lies not in removing Covetousness, casting that
Serpent out of Heaven (Mankind), and making
man to live in the light of Righteousness, not
in words only (as preachers do), but *in action*,
whereby the Creation shines in glory? I
affirm it.

" *Fourthly*, Whether is the King of Righteousness a respecter of persons, Yea or No? If you
say No, then who makes this difference, that
the elder brother should be lord of the land,
and the younger brother a slave and beggar?
I affirm, it was and is Covetousness since the
Fall, not the King of Righteousness before the

Fall, that made the difference; therefore, if you will be Preachers, hold forth the Law of Righteousness purely, and not the confused Law of Covetousness, which is the murderer. The Law of Righteousness would have every one to enjoy the benefit of his creation; that is, to have food and raiment by his labour freely in the land of his nativity; but Covetousness will have none to live free but he that hath the strongest arm of flesh; all others must be servants.

"*Fifthly*, Whether can a man have true peace, by walking in the Law of Covetousness and Self, as generally all do; or by walking in the Law of Universal Righteousness, doing as he would be done by? I affirm, there is no true peace, till men talk less, and live more actually in the power of Universal Righteousness. Then, you Preachers, lay aside your multitude of words, and your selfish doctrines; for you confound and delude the People.

"*Sixthly*, Whether does the King of Righteousness bid you love or hate your enemies? If you say, 'Love them'; then I demand of you, Why do some of you, in your pulpits, and elsewhere, stir up the People to beat, to imprison, put to

death, or banish, or not to buy and sell with those
that endeavour to restore the Earth to a Common
Treasury again? Surely, at the worst, you can
make them but your enemies; therefore, love
them, win them by love, do not hate them, they
do not hate you.

"*Seventhly*, Whether it be not a great breach
of the National Covenant to give two sorts of
people their freedom, that is, the Gentry and
Clergy, and deny it to the rest? I affirm, it is
a high breach; for man's laws make these two
sorts of people the Anti-Christian taskmasters
over the Common People: the one forcing the
People to give them Rent for the Earth, and to
work for hire for them; the other, which is the
Clergy, forcing a maintenance of Tithes from the
People—a practice which Christ, the Apostles,
and Prophets, never walked in. Therefore, surely,
you are the false Christs and false Prophets that
are risen up in these latter days.

"Thus, I have declared to you, and to all in
the whole world, what that Power of Life is
that is in me; and, knowing that the Spirit of
Righteousness does appear in many in this land
I desire all of you seriously, in love and humility,

to consider of this business of Public Community, which I am carried forth, in the power of love, and clear light of Universal Righteousness, to advance as much as I can; and I can do no other, the Law of Love in my heart does so constrain me : by reason whereof I am called fool and madman, and have many slandrous reports cast upon me, and meet with much fury from some covetous people; under all which my spirit is made patient, and is guarded with joy and peace. I hate none, I love all, I delight to see every one live comfortably, I would have none live in poverty, straits, or sorrows. Therefore, if you find any selfishness in this work, or discover anything that is destructive to the whole creation, I would that you would open your hearts as freely to me, in declaring my weakness to me, as I have been open-hearted in declaring that which I find and feel much life and strength in. But, if you see Righteousness in it, and that it holds forth the strength of Universal Love to all, without respect to persons, so that the Creator is honoured in the work of His hands; then own it, and justify it, and let the Power of Love have his freedom and glory.　　　JERRARD WINSTANLEY."

" *P.S.*—This letter was delivered by the Author's own hand to the General and Chief Officers; and they very mildly promised they would read it, and consider it."

But, needless to say, all this invincible logic was wasted on Fairfax, Cromwell, and the piously rapacious gang of Ironside Colonels whose sole aim it was to put down King and Cavalier, that they themselves might " live by kingly principles." " What," asked Oliver, with true squirearchal imperviousness, " is the purport of the levelling principle but to make the tenant as liberal a fortune as the landlord ? *I was by birth a gentleman.* You must cut these people in pieces or they will cut you in pieces," and the old Puritan savage was as good as his word.

In 1652, Oliver Cromwell, the Puritan " Man of Blood and Iron," stood at the parting of the ways. King Charles's head was no longer on his shoulders, and Oliver was simply the chief military servant of the Commonwealth as represented by the much " purged" remnant or " Rump" of the Long Parliament, whose throat he cut about a year later. He was still playing with Republicanism, just as Napoleon Bonaparte played with it when First Consul, and as Louis Napoleon played with it when President of the French Republic. He was the darling of the army jingoes, of the trader capitalists, and of the "Elect," or, as we should now perhaps say, the "Nonconformist Conscience."

The "Levellers"—the Social Democrats, or rather Communists, of the day—alone took an accurate measure of the about-to-be "Saviour of Society." In the spring of 1649, as has been seen, Winstanley and his friend Everard had led their company of "Diggers" to the waste land around St. George's Hill, Surrey, and had endeavoured to "digge the ground and sowe it with roots and beans." But this the Ironside colonels would not permit on any account, though the greedy pack of pious rascals were constantly "voting to one another" whatever remained of the Crown lands, Church lands, and the confiscated Malignants' lands. In vain had Winstanley asked them: "What profit has the Common People got from your victory over the King? The Nonconformist clergy and the gentry have got their freedom from the Bishops and the King. But

the Common People still are left servants to
work for them, like the Israelites under the
Egyptian taskmasters."

But I turn from the Digger's "Vindication of
Those whose Endeavour is Only to Make the
Earth a Common Treasury" to his masterpiece,
"The Law of Freedom in a Platform," with its
incisive and wholly unambiguous "Epistle Dedi-
catory to Oliver Cromwell." That Winstanley
did not underrate the importance of this production his own words abundantly testify :—

"It ('The Law of Freedom') was intended for
your (Cromwell's) view about two years ago; but
the disorder of the times caused me to lay it
aside, with a thought never to bring it to light.
I said I would not make it public; but this word
was like fire in my bones ever and anon: 'Thou
shalt not bury thy talents in the earth'; therefore
I was stirred up to give it a resurrection, and to
pick together as many of my scattered papers as I
could find, and to compile them into this method,
which I do here present to you, and do quiet my
own spirit."

It was Winstanley's conviction (which I entirely
share) that Cromwell had not the most elementary

notion " wherein what is kingly government and what is commonwealth's government differ," and he accordingly addressed himself to the herculean task of instructing not only him, but " all English-men my brethren, whether in Church-fellowship or not in Church-fellowship, and from them all the nations of the world." Thus :—

" When the Norman had conquered our fore-fathers, he took the free use of our English ground from them, and made them his servants. And God hath made you (Oliver) a successful instru-ment to cast out that conqueror, and to recover our land and liberties again by your victories, out of the Norman hand.

" That which is yet wanting on your part to be done is this : To see that the oppressor's power be cast out with his person, and to see that the free possession of the land and liberties be put into the hands of the oppressed commoners of England.

" And, now you have the power in your hands, you must do one of two things : First, either set the land free to the oppressed commoners, who assisted you and paid the army their wages : and then you will fulfil the Scriptures and your own engagements, and so take possession of your deserved honour. Or, secondly, you must only remove the conqueror's power out of the king's hand into other men's, maintaining the old laws still. And then your wisdom and honour are blasted for ever; and you will either lose yourself, or lay the foundation of greater slavery to posterity than you ever knew.

"You know that while the king was in the height of his oppressing power, the people only whispered in private chambers against him, but afterwards it was preached upon the house tops that he was a tyrant and a traitor to England's peace; and he had his overturn.

"The righteous power in the Creation is the same still. If you and those in power with you should be found walking in the king's steps, can you secure yourselves or posterities from an overturn? Surely no.

"The Spirit of the whole Creation (which is God) is about the reformation of the world, and He will go forward in His work; for, if He would not spare kings who have sat so long at His right hand, governing the world, neither will He regard *you* unless your ways be more righteous than the kings'."

The real foes to be overcome, Winstanley contended, are not so much the kings as the kings' allies—the Clergy with their "divine doctrine" (theology), and the Lawyers with their law:—

"Indeed, the main work of reformation lies in this: To reform the clergy, the lawyers, and the law; for all the complaints of the land are wrapped up within them three.

"Though their (the clergy's) preaching fill the minds of many with madness, contention, and unsatisfied doubting, because their imaginary and ungrounded doctrines cannot be understood by them, yet we must pay them large tithes for so doing! *This is oppression.*

"If we go to the lawyer we find him to sit in the conqueror's chair, though the kings be removed, maintaining the king's power to the height.

"If we look upon the customs of the law itself, it is the same it was in the king's days, only the *name* is altered; as if the commoners of England had paid their taxes, free-quarter, and shed their blood, not to reform, but to baptize the law into a new name from *Kingly law* to *State law;* and so as the sword pulls down kingly power with one hand, the king's old law builds up monarchy again with the other.

" Shall men of other nations say that, notwith-standing all those rare wits in the Parliament and Army of England, yet they could not reform the clergy, lawyer, and law, and must needs establish all as the kings left them ?

" Will not this blast our honour, and make all monarchical members laugh in their sleeves to see the government of our Commonwealth still built upon the kingly laws and principles ?

" I have asked divers soldiers what they fought for : they answered they could not tell ; and it is very true indeed they cannot tell, if the monarchical law is established without reformation."

Here the " Digger " goes to the very root of the causes which have stultified alike all the three great modern revolutions—the English, the American, and the French. The rank and file never knew " what they fought for." They were imposed upon by names, with the results we to-day know to our cost. And foremost among the impostors was Oliver Cromwell, the idol whom Carlyle, Dr. Gardiner, Frederic Harrison, Allanson Picton, Lord Rosebery, and so many more men of light and leading would have us all fall down and worship. Alas, alas! "with how little wisdom this world is governed!" The one poor wise man— "Digger" Winstanley—who by his wisdom clearly discerned how the city was to be delivered, is unremembered to this day.

But let us follow Cromwell's mentor a little further. Had our seventeenth-century Tolstoy the hollow capitalistic republics of the United States and France in his seer's vision of the closing decade of the nineteenth century when he wrote—

"For you must either establish Commonwealth's freedom in power, making provision for every one's peace, which is righteousness, or else you must set up Monarchy again. Monarchy is twofold, either for one king to reign, or for many to rule by kingly principles; for the king's power lies in his laws, not in his name. And if either one king rules, or many rule by king's principles, much murmuring, grudges, troubles, and quarrels may and will arise among the oppressed people on every gained opportunity."

Every human being, according to Winstanley, is possessed of unalienable "Creation-Rights," or what a hundred and fifty years later Thomas

Paine immortalised as the "Rights of Man."
Among these the chief is complete immunity from
Rent, which is none other than " club-law ":—

" And is not this a slavery, say the people, that
though there be land enough in England to maintain ten times as many people as are in it, yet
some must beg of their brethren, or work in hard
drudgery for day wages for them, or starve, or
steal, and so be hanged out of the way, as men
not fit to live on the earth ?   Before they are
suffered to plant the waste land for a livelihood,
they must pay rent to their brethren for it.   Well,
this is a burthen the Creation groans under; and
the subjects (so called) have not their birthright-
freedom granted them from their brethren, who
hold it from them by club law, but not by
righteousness."

But with all his inexorable logic Winstanley
was no Marxian or State Socialist.   He was
a Voluntary, rather than an Involuntary Co-
operator; "for all Commonwealth's rulers are
servants to, not lords and kings over, the People."
Coercion he abominated, except for the gravest
offences against the Commonwealth when once
firmly established :—

"I do not say nor desire that every one shall be compelled to practise this Commonwealth's Government; for the spirits of some will be enemies at first, though afterwards they will prove the most cordial and true friends thereunto. Yet I desire that the Commonwealth's land . . . may be set free to all that have lent assistance of person or purse to obtain it; and to all that are willing to come in to the practice of this Government, and be obedient to the laws thereof. And for others who are not willing, let them stay in the way of buying and selling, which is the law of the conqueror, till they be willing."

Let it be here specially noted that " the way of buying and selling is the law of the conqueror," and that " the great Lawgiver in Commonwealth's Government is the Spirit of Universal Righteousness dwelling in mankind, now rising up to teach every one to do to another as he would have another do to him."

" Is not buying and selling a righteous law ? No, it is the law of the conqueror, but not the righteous Law of Creation. How can that be righteous which is a cheat ? For is not this a common practice, when one hath a bad horse or a cow, or any bad commodity, he will send it to the market to cheat some simple, plain-hearted man or other, and when he comes home will laugh at his neighbour's hurt, and much more.

"When mankind began to buy and sell, then did they fall from innocency; for then they began to oppress and cozen one another of their Creation birthright: as, for example, if the land belong to three persons, and two of them buy and sell the earth, and the third give no consent, his right is taken from him, and his posterity is engaged in a war.

"When the earth was first bought and sold, many gave no consent. Therefore, this buying and selling did bring in, and still doth bring in, discontents and wars, which have plagued mankind sufficiently for so doing. And the nations of the world will never learn to beat their swords into ploughshares, and their spears into pruning-hooks, and leave off warring, until this cheating device of buying and selling be cast out among the rubbish of kingly power."

Winstanley's gratitude to the "pious founder" was small:

"But shall not one man be richer than another?

"There is no need of that; for riches make men vainglorious, proud, and to oppress their brethren; and are the occasion of wars.

"No man can be rich, but he must be rich either by his own labours or by the labours of other men helping him. If a man have no help from his neighbour, he shall never gather an estate of hundreds and thousands a year. If other men help him to work, then are these riches his neighbours' as well as his, for they be the fruit of other men's labours as well as his own.

"But all rich men live at ease, feeding and clothing themselves by the labours of other men, not by their own, which is their shame and not their nobility; for it is a more blessed thing to give than to receive. But rich men receive all they have from the labourer's hand, and what they give, they give away other men's labours, not their own; therefore they are not righteous actors in the earth."

Many, indeed most, experiments in practical Communism have been shipwrecked on the rock of *sex,* but Winstanley foresaw the danger and avoided it:

"Shall every man count his neighbour's house as his own, and live together as one family?

"No; though the earth and storehouses be common to every family, yet every family shall live apart as they now do; and every man's house, wife, children, and furniture for ornament of his house, or anything which he hath fetched from the storehouses, or provided for the necessary use of his family, is all a *propriety* of that family for the peace thereof."

The following I feel to be a trifle subversive of "Law and Order," and even somewhat personal, but I am not in a quarrelsome mood:—

"Shall we have no lawyers?

"There is no need of them, for there is to be no buying and selling; neither any need to expound laws; for the bare letter of the law shall be both judge and lawyer, trying every man's actions.

"But there are to be officers chosen yearly in every Parish, to see the Laws executed to the letter; so that there will be no long work in trying of offences, as it is under Kingly Government, to get the Lawyers' Money, and to enslave the Commoners to the Conqueror's prerogative Law or Will. The sons of contention, Simeon and Levi, must not bear Rule in a free Commonwealth.

"At first view, you may say this is a strange Government, but I pray judge nothing before trial. Lay this Platform of Commonwealth's Government in one scale, and lay Monarchy or Kingly Government in the other scale, and see which gives true weight to righteous Freedom and Peace. There is no middle path between these two; for a man must be either a free and true Commonwealth's man, or a Monarchical tyrannical Royalist.

"If any say, This will bring Poverty, surely they mistake: for there will be plenty of all earthly Commodities, with less labour and trouble than now it is under Monarchy. There will be no want, for every man may keep as plentiful a house as he will, and never run into debt, for common stock pays for all.

"If you say, Some will live idle; I answer, No: it will make idle persons to become Workers (as is declared in the Platform): There shall be neither Beggar nor Idle Person.

"If you say, This will make men quarrel and fight; I answer, No: it will turn swords into ploughshares, and settle such peace in the Earth, as Nations shall learn war no more. Indeed the Government of Kings is a breeder of Wars, because men, being put into the straits of Poverty, are moved to fight for Liberty, and to take one another's Estates from them, and to obtain Mastery. Look into all Armies and see what they do more but make some poor, some rich; put some into freedom, and others into bondage: And is not this a plague among Mankind?

"I have been somewhat large, because I could not contract myself into lesser volume, having so many things to speak of.

"Yet I desire that the Commonwealth's Land, which is the ancient Commons and Waste Land, and the Lands newly got in by the Armies' victories, out of the oppressor's hands, Parks, Forests, Chases, and the like, may be set free to all who lent assistance, either of person or purse, to obtain it; and to all that are willing to come into the practice of this Government, and be obedient to the Laws thereof. And for others, who are not willing, let them stay in the way of Buying and

Selling, which is the Law of the Conqueror, till
they be willing.

"And so I leave this in your hand, humbly pros-
trating myself and it before you, and remain,

    "A true Lover of Commonwealth's

        Government, Peace, and Freedom,

          JERRARD WINSTANLEY.

"*Nov.* 5, 1651."

Having disposed of Cromwell, the "Digger" next
addresses himself in characteristic fashion—

"TO THE FRIENDLY, UNBIASSED READER.

"To prevent thy hasty rashness, I have given
thee a short compendium of the whole.

"First, Thou Knowest that the Earth in all
Nations is governed by *buying and selling*, for
all the laws of Kings have relation thereunto.

"Now this Platform following declares to thee
the Government of the Earth without buying
and selling, and the Laws are the Laws of a free
and peaceable Commonwealth, which casts out
everything that offends.

"The Earth shall be planted, and the fruits
reaped, and carried into Store-houses by Common

Assistance of every Family: The Riches of the Store-houses shall be the Common Stock to every Family. There shall be no Idle Person or Beggar in the land.

" Reader, here is a trial for thy sincerity: Thou shalt have no want of food, raiment, or freedom among Brethren in this way propounded. See now if thou canst be content, as the Scriptures say, 'having food and raiment therewith be content,' and grudge not to let thy brother have the same with thee.

" Dost thou pray and fast for Freedom and give God thanks for it? Why, know that God is not partial; for if thou pray, it must be for Freedom to all; and if thou give thanks, it must be because freedom covers all people, for this will prove a lasting Peace.

" Every one is ready to say, I fight for my country; and what I do I do for the good of my country. Well, let it appear now that thou hast fought and acted for thy country's Freedom. But if, when thou hast power to settle Freedom in thy country, thou takest possession of the Earth into thine own hands, and makest thy brother work for thee, as the Kings did, thou hast fought and acted for thyself, not for thy country; and here thy inside hypocrisy is discovered.

" But here take notice, That Common Freedom, which is the Rule I would have practised and not talked about, was thy pretence; but particular Freedom to thyself was thy intent. Amend, or else thou shalt be shamed, when Knowledge doth spread to cover the Earth, even as the waters cover the seas.

" And so farewell."

From all economists, past or present, Jerrard Winstanley, the " Digger," easily carries off the palm for completeness and intelligibility. His " Commonwealth's Government " involves no fearsome Marxian " Theory of Value," nor even so much as a Georgian " Single Tax on Land Values." Why? Because the deadliest of crimes consists, as has been seen, in " the Conqueror's Law of Buying and Selling "—buying and selling of lands, commodities, or services. The contract of purchase and sale is a *malum per se*, and, therefore, a thing absolutely forbidden in Winstanley's " Law of Freedom in a Platform." Consequently Money, Rent, Taxes,

Interest, Wages, all become at a blow meaningless or obsolete terms. What has the Cobden Club to say to this?

LAWS AGAINST BUYING AND SELLING.

"If any man entice another to buy and sell, and he who is enticed doth not yield, but makes it known to the Overseer, the enticer shall lose his freedom for twelve months, and the Overseer shall give words of commendation to him that refused the enticement, before all the Congregation, for his faithfulness to the *commonwealth's peace.*

"If any do buy or sell the earth or fruits thereof, unless it be to or with strangers, *according to the Law of Navigation,* they shall be both put to death as traitors to the peace of the Commonwealth; because it brings in kingly bondage again, and is the occasion of all quarrels and oppressions.

"He or she who calls the earth his and not his brother's, shall be set upon a stool, with those words written on his forehead, before all the congregation; and afterwards be made a servant for twelve months under the Taskmaster. If he quarrel or seek by secret persuasion, or open rising in arms, to set up such kingly propriety, he shall be put to death.

"No man shall either give hire or take hire for his work, for this brings in kingly bondage. He that gives and he that takes hire for work shall both lose their freedom, and become servants for twelve months under the Taskmaster."

And here it may be as well that the reader should be made acquainted with the "Laws of Navigation," for the "Digger" overlooks no difficulty and no contingency.

Laws of Navigation.

"Because other nations as yet own monarchy, and will *buy* and *sell ;* therefore it is convenient, for the peace of our Commonwealth, that our ships do transport our English goods, and exchange for theirs, and conform to the customs of other nations in buying and selling. Provided that what goods our ships carry out they shall be the Commonwealth's goods, and all their trading with other nations shall be upon the common stock to enrich the storehouses."

As in ancient communistic Peru, so in Win-

stanley's Commonwealth, no medium of exchange
being needed, gold and silver have no other use
than as objects of utility or ornament:—

LAWS FOR SILVER AND GOLD.

" The righteous Spirit of the whole Creation did
never enact such a law that, unless weak and simple
men did go from England to the East Indies
(Johannesburg) and fetch silver and gold in their
hands to their brethren, and give it them for their
goodwill to let them plant the earth, the earth
should *not* be planted and enjoyed.   Therefore,
there shall be no other use for silver and gold
in the Commonwealth than to make dishes and
other necessaries for the ornament of houses, as
now there is use made of brass, pewter, iron, or
any other metal."

But of all regulations the most important
are:—

THE LAWS OF STOREHOUSES.

" There shall be storehouses in all places, both
in the country and in the cities, to which all
the fruits of the earth, and other works made
by tradesmen, shall be brought and thence de-

livered out again to particular families, and to every one as they want for their use; or else to be transported by ship to other lands in exchange for those things which our land will not or does not afford.

"And as every one works to advance the common stock, so every one shall have a free use of every commodity in the storehouse for his pleasure and comfortable livelihood, without buying or selling, or restraint from any."

THERE ARE TWO SORTS OF STOREHOUSES, GENERAL AND PARTICULAR.

"General storehouses are such as receive all commodities in the gross, as all barns and places to lay corn and the fruits of the earth at first reaping.

"Particular storehouses, or shops, to which the tradesmen shall bring their particular works; iron instruments to the iron shops, hats to shops appointed for them, and the like.

"And all these storehouses shall be orderly kept by such as shall be brought up to be waiters therein.

"They shall receive in, as into a storehouse, and

deliver out again freely, as out of a common store-house, when particular persons or families come for anything they need, as now they do by buying and selling under kingly government.

" Come hither now, all you (Cromwellian crowd) who challenge your brethren to deny (as deniers of) Christ, as though you were the only men that love Christ and would be true to Him. Here is a trial of your love. Can you be as ready to obey the law of liberty, which is the command of Christ, as you would have others to obey your kingly laws of bondage ?

" Well, here is life and death set before you, take which you will; but know that unless your right-eousness exceed the righteousness of the kingly and lordly Scribes and Pharisees, you shall never enjoy true peace in your spirit."

The " Digger," it is noteworthy, did not believe in any " project of law " until after its formal sanction by vote of the people. In a word, before the " blessed word " Referendum was ever heard of, Winstanley entertained the most wholesome suspicion of the " Elected Person," and strove to confine his activities to purely administrative functions. *Secundum naturam vivere* was the old anti-Puritan's maxim, but according to the higher or rational nature of man, and not to the lower or merely animal. He asks:—

WHAT IS LAW IN GENERAL?

"Law is a rule, whereby man and other creatures are governed in their actions for the preservation of the common peace. And this law is twofold:

"First, it is the power of life (called the law of nature within the creatures), which does move both man and beast in their actions; or that causes grass, trees, corn, and all plants to grow in their several seasons. And whatsoever anybody does, he does it as he is moved by this inward law. And this law of nature moves two-fold—*rationally and irrationally*.

"A man by this inward law is guided to actions of generation and present consent rashly, through a greedy self-love, without any consideration, like foolish children, or like brute beasts: by reason whereof much hurt many times follows the body. And this is called the *law in the members* warring against the *law of the mind*.

"Or when there is an inward watchful oversight of all motions to action, considering the end and effects of such actions, that there do no excess in diet, in speech, or in action, break forth, to the prejudice of a man's self or others. And this is called *the light in man, the reasonable power, or the law of the mind.*

"And this rises up in the heart by an experienced observation of that peace and trouble which such and such words, thoughts, and actions bring the man into. And this is called the *record on high;* for it is a record in a man's heart *above* the former unreasonable power. And it is called *the witness or testimony of a man's own conscience.*"

THERE ARE TWO ROOTS OF LAW.

"(1.) Common Preservation.

"(2.) Self-Preservation.

"Common Preservation and Peace is the Foundation Rule of all Government; and, therefore, if any will preach or practise Fundamental Truths or Doctrine, here you may see where the Foundation thereof lies.

"Self-Preservation is the Root of the Tree, Tyranny, and the Law of Unrighteousness, and all particular Kingly Laws found out by Covetous

Policy to enslave one brother to another, whereby bondage, tears, sorrows and poverty are brought upon men, are all but the boughs and branches of the Tree, Tyranny; and such Officers as are of these are fallen from true Magistracy, and are no members thereof, but the Members of Tyranny, who is the Devil and Satan.

" And, indeed, this Tyranny is the cause of all Wars and Troubles, and of the removal of the Government of the Earth out of one hand into another, so often as it is in all Nations.

" For if Magistrates had a care to cherish the peace and liberties of the Common People, and see them set free from Oppression, they might sit in the Chair of Government and never be disturbed.

" But when their sitting is altogether to advance their own interest, and to forget the afflictions of their brethren that are under bondage; this is a forerunner of their own downfall, and oftentime proves the plague of the whole Land.

ALL COMMONWEALTH OFFICERS TO BE CHOSEN.

" A true Commonwealth's Officer is not to step into the place of Magistracy by policy or violent force, as all Kings and Conquerors do, but is to be a chosen one, by them who are in necessity, and who judge him fit for that work.

" *Firstly*.—In the Family the Father is a Commonwealth's Officer, because the Necessity of the Young Children choose him by joint consent and not otherwise.

" *Secondly*. — In the bigger Family, called a Parish, doth the Necessity of Common Peace move the whole body of the Parish to choose two, three, or more, within that circuit, to be their Overseers, to cause the unruly ones (for whom only the Law was added) to be subject to the Law or Rule, that so peace may be observed among them in the planting of the Earth, reaping the fruits, and quiet enjoyment.

" *Thirdly*.—In every County, Shire, or Land, wherein the Families are increased to a larger Commonwealth, the necessity of the People moves them still to choose more Overseers to preserve the Common peace.

" So that all true Officers are chosen Officers, and when they act to satisfy the necessity of them who choose them, then they are faithful and righteous servants to that Commonwealth, and there is a rejoicing in the City.

" But when Officers do take the possessions of the Earth into their own hands, lifting themselves up thereby to be Lords over their Masters, the People who choose them ; and will not suffer the People to plant the Earth, and reap the fruits of their livelihood, unless they will hire the Land of them, or work for day-wages for them, that they may live in ease and plenty, and not work.

" These Officers are fallen from true Magistracy of a Commonwealth, and they do not act righteously ; and because of this, tears and sorrows, poverty and bondages are known among Mankind ; and now that City mourns.

Annual Elections.

" Nature tells us, *That if water stand long it corrupts ;* whereas running water keeps sweet, and is fit for Common use.

" Therefore, as the necessity of Common Preservation moves the People to frame a Law, and to choose Officers to see the Law obeyed, that they may live in peace :

" So doth the same Necessity bid the People, and cries aloud in the Ears and Eyes of England to choose *new* Officers, and to remove the old ones, and to choose State-Officers every year.

" Have we not experience in these days, that some Officers of the Commonwealth are grown so mossy for want of removing, that they will hardly speak to an old acquaintance, if he be an inferior man, though they were very familiar before these wars began ?   And what hath occasioned this distance among friends and brethren but too long continuance in places of honour, greatness, and riches ?

Who are not Fit to Choose and to be Chosen Officers of the Commonwealth.

" *Firstly*.—All uncivil livers, as drunkards, quarrellers, fearful ignorant men who dare not speak truth lest they anger other men ; likewise all who are wholly given to pleasure and sports, or men who are full of talk ; all these are empty of substance, and cannot be experienced men, therefore, not fit to be Chosen Officers in a Commonwealth, yet they may have a voice in the choosing.

" *Secondly*.—All those who are interested in Monarchical Power and Government, ought neither to choose nor to be Chosen Officers to manage

Commonwealth's affairs. And these are of two sorts :—

"First, such as have lent money to maintain the King's Army, or in that Army have been soldiers to fight against the recovering of Common Freedom, these are neither to choose nor be chosen.

"Second, all those who have been so hasty to buy and sell the Commonwealth's Land, and so to entangle it in a new accompt, ought neither to choose nor be Chosen Officers.

"For there is neither Reason nor Equity, that a few men should go away with that Land-Freedom which the whole Commoners have paid Taxes, Free-quarter, and wasted their Estates, Healths, and Blood, to purchase out of Bondage, and many of them are in want of a comfortable livelihood. What greater ignorance could be declared by Officers than to sell away the purchased Land from the Purchasers, or from part of them into the hands of particular men to uphold Monarchical Principles ?

"Yet seeing but few of the Parliament's friends understand their Common Freedoms, though they own the name *Commonwealth*, therefore, the

Parliamentary Party ought to bear with the ignorance of the King's Party, because they are brethren, and not make them servants, though for the present they be suffered neither to choose nor to be Chosen Officers, lest their ignorant spirit of revenge break out in them to interrupt our Common Peace.

WHO, THEN, ARE FIT TO BE COMMONWEALTH'S OFFICERS?

"Why, truly, choose such as have a long time given testimony by their actions to be promoters of Common Freedom, whether they be Members in Church Fellowship, or not in Church Fellowship, for all are one in Christ.

". . . Choose men of Courage, who are not afraid to speak the Truth, for this is the shame of many in England at this day, they are drowned in dunghill mud of slavish fear of men; these are covetous men, not fearing God, and their portion is to be cast without the City of Peace among the Dogs.

"Choose Officers out of the number of those men that are above forty years of age, for these are most likely to be experienced men; and all these are likely to be men of Courage, dealing truly, and hating Covetousness.

"And if you choose men thus principled, who are poor men, as times go; for the Conqueror's Power hath made many a righteous man a poor man; then allow them a yearly Maintenance from the Common Stock, until such time as a Commonwealth's Freedom is established, for then there will be no need of such allowances.

"What is the reason that most people are so ignorant of their Freedoms, and so unfit to be Chosen Commonwealth's Officers?

"Because the old King Clergy, that are seated in Parishes for lucre of Tythes, are continually distilling their blind principles into the People, and do thereby nurse up Ignorance in them, for they observe the bent of the People's minds, and make sermons to please the sickly minds of ignorant people, to preserve their own riches and esteem among a charmed, befooled, and besotted people.

OF PARTICULAR COMMONWEALTH'S LAWS.

"1. The bare letter of the law sufficeth.

"2. He who adds to or diminishes this law shall lose his office.

" 3. No man shall administer the law for money or reward under pain of death."

LAWS FOR PLANTING OF THE EARTH.

" Every household shall keep all instruments and tools for the tillage of the earth.

" If any shall refuse to assist in the work the Overseers shall ask the reason, and if it be sickness, or any other distemper that hinders them, they are freed from such service; if mere idleness keep them back, they are to suffer punishment according to the Laws against Idleness."

LAWS AGAINST IDLENESS.

" If any refuse to learn a trade, or refuse to work in seed-time or harvest, or to be a waiter in storehouses, and yet will feed and clothe himself with other men's labours, the Overseers shall first admonish him privately; if he continue idle he shall be reproved openly before all the people by the Overseers, and shall be forebore with for a month after this reproof. If he still continue idle he shall be delivered into the Taskmaster's hands, who shall set him to work for twelve months, or till he submit to order."

The considerations of space forbid me to define their functions, but here are the

OFFICERS' NAMES IN A FREE COMMONWEALTH.

    I. In family, the Father.

    II. In town, city, or parish :—

        (1) The Peacemaker.

        (2) The Fourfold Overseer (*a*) for peace preservation ; (*b*) for trades—apprenticeship; (*c*) for tradesmen to bring their work to stores ; (*d*) for all over sixty to be General Overseers.

        (3) Soldier.

        (4) Taskmaster.

        (5) Executioner.

    III. In a whole land :—

        (1) Parliament.

        (2) Commonwealth's Ministry (clergy).

        (3) Army.

" All these officers are like links of a chain ; and the rule of right government being thus observed, may make a whole land, nay, the whole fabric of the earth, to become one family of mankind, and one well-governed Commonwealth."

Of Education.

" To prevent the dangerous events (outcome) of idleness in Scholars, it is reason that, after Children have been brought up at Schools, to ripen their wits they shall then be set to such Trades, Arts and Sciences, as their bodies are capable of, and therein continue till they come to be forty years of age.

" Then from forty to fourscore, if they live so long, which is the degree of manhood and old age; they shall be freed from all labour and work, unless they will themselves. And from this degree of Mankind shall be chosen all Officers and Overseers, to see the Laws of the Commonwealth observed.

What Trades should Men be Brought Up in.

" There are five Fountains of Industry :—

" *First.*—(*a.*) Husbandry (*b.*) Gardening.

" *Second.*—' Mineral Employments.'

" *Third.*—Cattle-Tending.

" *Fourth.*—Right Ordering of Timber Trees.

" *Fifth.*—To find out the Secrets of Nature.

" And all these five fountains there is knowledge in the practice, and it is good.

" But there is Traditional Knowledge, which is attained by reading, or by the instruction of others, and not practical, and this is not good.

" The latter is no knowledge, but a show of knowledge, like a parrot which speaks words, but he knows not what he saith.

OF SICKNESS.

" If any persons be sick or wounded the Chirurgeons, who are trained up in the Knowledge of Herbs and Minerals, and know how to apply plaisters or physic, shall go when they are sent for to any who need their help but require no reward, because the Common Stock is the public pay for every man's labours."

Well, well, Cromwell's day is past for ever, in spite of the Rosebery resuscitation, and Winstanley's is not yet. Albeit, there is immeasurably more true wisdom in the "Digger's" unremembered pages than is to be found in all the " Protector's " " Letters and Speeches," even with the miraculous exegesis of Carlyle thrown in. Like Jesus, the Son of Sirach, Winstanley fully apprehended the

great truth that " Fraud ever sticketh between
Buying and Selling as mortar between stones."
Again and again he reverts to it, and I, for one,
back him *contra mundum*.   In the institution or
contract of Purchase and Sale of Lands, Commodities, and Services, lurks the root of all social
and moral evil :—

The Nursery of Cheaters.

" And so this Proverb is true, *Plain dealing is
a jewel, but he who uses it shall die a beggar.*
And why ?

" Because this *Buying* and *Selling* is a Nursery
of Cheaters.   It is the Law of the Conqueror,
and the Righteousness of the Scribes and
Pharisees, who both killed Christ and hindered
His Resurrection, as much as darkness can put
out Light.

"Therefore, there shall be no *Buying* and
Selling in a Free Commonwealth, neither shall
any one hire his brother to work for him.

" The Earth is to be planted, and the fruits
reaped and carried into Barns and Storehouses
by the assistance of every family.   And if any
Man or Family want Corn or other provision,

they may go to the Storehouses and fetch without Money. If you want a horse to ride, go into the fields in summer, or to the common stables in winter, and receive one from the keepers, and when your journey is performed bring him where you had him without money.

" Well now, God and Christ have enacted an everlasting Law, which is Love; not only one another of your own mind, but love your enemies too, such as are not of your mind; and having food and raiment, therewith be content.

" A man had better to have no body, than to have no food for it; therefore this restraining of the Earth from brethren by brethren is oppression and bondage; but the free enjoyment thereof is true Freedom.

" True Freedom lies where a man receives his nourishment and preservation, and that is in the use of the Earth. For as Man is compounded of the four Materials of the Creation, *Fire, Water, Earth,* and *Air,* so is he preserved by the compounded of these four, which are the fruits of the Earth, and he cannot live without them. For take away the free use of these, and the body languishes, the Spirit is brought into bondage, and at length departs, and ceaseth his motional action in the body.

"All that a man labours for, saith Solomon (Eccles. ii. 24), is this, That he may enjoy the free use of the Earth with the fruits thereof.

"Do not the Ministers preach for maintenance in the Earth? The Lawyers plead causes to get possession of the Earth? Doth not the soldier fight for the Earth? And does not the Landlord require Rent, that he may live in the fulness of the Earth by the labour of his Tenants?

"And so from the thief on the highway to the King who sits upon the Throne, does not every one strive, either by force of Arms or Secret Cheats, to get the possessions of the Earth one from another, because they see their Freedom lies in plenty, and their bondage in poverty?

"Surely, then, oppressing Lords of Manors, exacting Landlords, and Tithe-takers, may as well say, Their brethren shall not breathe in the air, nor enjoy warmth in their bodies, nor have the moist waters to fall upon them in showers, unless they will pay them Rent for it, as to say, Their brethren shall not work upon Earth, nor eat the fruits thereof, unless they will hire that liberty from them. For he that takes it upon him to restrain his brothers from the liberty of the one may upon the same ground restrain him from the liberty of all four; viz., Fire, Water, Earth, and Air.

" I speak now in relation between the oppressor and the oppressed; the inward bondages of the mind, as covetousness, pride, hypocrisy, envy, sorrow, fears, desperation, and madness are all occasioned by outward bondage that one sort of people lay upon another.

"And thus far natural experience makes it good, That true Freedom lies in the free enjoyment of the Earth."

It will thus be seen that the " Digger " found in "outward bondage," or, as we should now perhaps say, in "environment," the seeds of all personal immoralities. He laughed at the Puritan "Elect." As the Rev. Thomas Hancock, of Harrow-on-the-Hill, has justly observed :—

" His theory of Social Reformation had its basis in an essentially modern and profoundly Anti-Puritan conception. He conceived of God, like the Alexandrian Fathers of the Church, as the Eternal *Reason,* and of Man and the whole

Creation as the products of that perfect Reason. Personal and social life, the Conscience and the State, as he contended, had fallen or apostatised from Reason, and, consequently, no actual reformation was possible except by the personal and social return of men to the original formation in which God had constituted them."

Those who may desire a fuller comprehension of the "Digger's" spiritual standpoint will find ample material in:—1. "Breaking of the Day of God"; 2. "Mystery of God Concerning the Whole Creation"; 3. "The Saint's Paradise"; 4. "Truth Lifting up its Head against Scandals"; 5. "The New Law of Righteousness," &c., all erstwhile "Sold by Giles Calvert, at the Black Spread-Eagle, at the West End of St. Paul's."

Government is twofold: Kingly and Commonwealth's. The one is apostate from Eternal Reason, the other is in harmony with it.

KINGLY AND COMMONWEALTH'S GOVERNMENTS CONTRASTED.

" Kingly Government governs the Earth by the cheating Art of Buying and Selling, and take this Government at its best, it is but a diseased Government, full of confusion. If it had not a Club Law to support it, there would be no order in it, because it is the covetous and proud will of a Conqueror enslaving a conquered people.

"This Kingly Government calls itself the Lord God of the whole Creation, for it makes one brother to pay rent to another brother for the use of the water, earth, and air, or else it will not suffer him by his laws and lawyers to live above ground but in beggary, and yet it will be called righteous.

"And this was the rise of Kingly power; first by policy, drawing the people from a common enjoyment of the Earth to the Crafty Art of Buying and Selling; secondly, to advance itself by the power of the sword when the Art of Buying and Selling had made them quarrel among themselves.

"Commonwealth's Government governs the Earth without Buying and Selling, and thereby becomes the restorer of ancient peace and freedom; makes provision for the oppressed, the weak, and the simple, as well as for the rich, the wise, and the strong; beats swords and spears into pruning-hooks and ploughs, and makes both elder and younger brothers freemen in the earth.

"Where oppression lieth upon brethren by brethren, that is no Commonwealth's Government, but the Kingly Government still; and the Mystery of Iniquity hath taken that Peacemaker's name (O Cromwell!) to be a cloak to hide his subtile covetousness, pride, and oppression under.

"The great lawgiver in Commonwealth's Government is the Spirit of Universal Righteousness dwelling in mankind, now rising up to teach every one to do to another as he would have another to do to him, and is no respecter of persons, and this Spirit hath been killed by the Pharisaical kingly spirit of self-love, and hath been buried in the dunghill of that enmity for many years past.

"*In that Nation, where this Commonwealth's Government shall be first established, there shall be abundance of peace and plenty, and all Nations of the Earth shall come flocking hither to see its beauty, and to learn the ways thereof; and the Law shall go forth from that Zion; and the Word of the Lord from that Jerusalem, which shall govern the whole earth*" (Micah iv. 1, 2).

Finally, I would ask the "clergy of all denominations," and particularly the "Nonconformist Conscience," carefully to ponder the fol-

lowing *morceaux,* which I have specially excerpted
for their benefit:—

COMMONWEALTH'S CHRISTIAN MINISTRY.

" If the earth were set free from kingly bondage,
so that every one might be sure of a free livelihood, and if this liberty were granted, then many
secrets of God and His works in nature would be
made public, which men nowadays keep secret to
get a living by; so that this kingly bondage is the
cause of the spreading of ignorance in the earth.
But when Commonwealth's freedom is established,
then will *knowledge cover the earth as the waters
cover the seas,* and not till then.

" He who is chosen Minister for the year shall not
be the only man to make sermons or speeches (on
the day of rest from labour); but every one who
hath any experience, and is able to speak of any
art or language, or of the nature of the heavens
above or the earth below, shall have free liberty
to speak when they offer themselves, and in a
civil manner desire an audience; yet he who is
the Reader (for the year) may have his liberty to
speak too, but not to assume all the power to himself, as the proud and ignorant clergy have done

who have bewitched all the world by their subtile covetousness and pride.

" And every one who speaks of any herb, plant, art, or nature of mankind is required to *speak nothing by imagination,* but what he hath found out by his own industry and observation in trial.

" And thus to speak, or thus to read the Law of Nature (or God) as He hath written His name in everybody, is to speak the truth as Jesus Christ spake it, giving to everything its own weight and measure.

" Ay, but, saith the zealous but ignorant professor (of religion)—

" ' *This is a low and carnal ministry indeed. This leads men to know nothing but the knowledge of the earth, and the secrets of nature; but we are to look after spiritual and heavenly things.*'

" I answer—

" To know the secrets of Nature is to know the works of God, and to know the works of God within the Creation is to know God Himself; for God dwells in every visible work or body.

" And, indeed, if you would know spiritual things, it is to know how the Spirit or Power of Wisdom and Life, causing motion or growth, dwells within, and governs both the several bodies of the stars and planets in the heavens above; and the several bodies of the earth below, as grass, plants, fishes, beasts, birds, and mankind; for to reach God beyond the Creation, or to know what He will be to a man after the man is dead, if any otherwise than to scatter him into his essences of fire, water, earth, and air, of which he is compounded, is a knowledge beyond the line or capacity of man to attain to while he lives in his compounded body."

In dealing with Theology — " Divining Doctrine " he contemptuously calls it—as contradistinguished from Religion or the Faith of Christ, Winstanley is all over Tolstoyan :—

" DIVINING DOCTRINE.

" This divining Doctrine, which you call 'spiritual and heavenly things,' is the thief and the robber that comes to spoil the vineyard of a man's peace, and does not enter at the door, but climbs up another way. They who preach this divining Doctrine are the murtherers of many a poor heart, who is bashful and simple, and cannot speak for himself, but keeps his thoughts to himself. This

divining spiritual doctrine is a cheat; for while
men are gazing up to heaven, imagining after a
happiness or fearing a hell after they are dead,
their eyes are put out, and they see not what is
their birthrights, and what is to be done by them
here on earth while they are living. This is the
filthy dreamer and the cloud without rain.

" And indeed the subtle Clergy do know that if
they can but charm the people by their divining
Doctrine to look after heavenly riches and glory
after they are dead, that then they shall easily be
the inheritors of the earth, and have the deceived
people to be their servants.

" This divining Doctrine, which you call spiritual and heavenly, was not the Doctrine of Christ,
for His words were pure knowledge. They were
words of life; for He said *He spoke what He had
seen with his Father*, for He had the knowledge
of the Creation, and spoke *as everything was*.

" And this Divinity came in, after Christ, to
darken His Knowledge; and it is the language of
the Mystery of Iniquity and Antichrist, whereby
the covetous, ambitious, and serpentine spirit
cozens the plain-hearted of his portions of the
Earth.

" But surely Light is so broke out that it will cover the Earth, so that the Divinity Charmers shall say, *The People will not hear the voice of our charming, charm we never so wisely.* And all the Priests and Clergy, and Preachers of these 'spiritual and heavenly things,' as they call them, shall take up the lamentation, which is their portion: *Alas, alas, that great City Babylon, that mighty City Divinity, which hath filled the whole Earth with her sorcery, and deceived all people, so that the whole world wondered after this Beast; how is it fallen, and how is her judgment come upon her in one hour?* (Rev. xviii. 10)."

APPENDIX A

[From the *Clarke Papers*]

THE DIGGERS' SONG

BY JERRARD WINSTANLEY (1649)

YOU noble Diggers all, stand up now, stand up now,
   You noble Diggers all, stand up now,
The waste land to maintain, seeing Cavaliers by
     name
Your digging do disdain and persons all defame,
          Stand up now, stand up now.

Your houses they pull down, stand up now, stand
     up now,
   Your houses they pull down, stand up now;
Your houses they pull down to fright poor men in
     town,
But the gentry must come down, and the poor
     shall wear the crown.
         Stand up now, Diggers all !

With spades and hoes and plows, stand up now,
    stand up now,
  With spades and plows and hoes, stand up
    now,
Your freedom to uphold, seeing Cavaliers are
    bold
To kill you if they could, and rights from you
    withhold.
              Stand up now, Diggers all!

Their self-will is their law, stand up now, stand up
    now,
  Their self-will is their law, stand up now;
Since tyranny came in they count it now no sin
To make a gaol a gin, to starve poor men therein.
              Stand up now, stand up now.

The gentry are all round, stand up now, stand up
    now,
  The gentry are all round, stand up now;
The gentry are all round, on each side they are
    found,
Their wisdom's so profound to cheat us of our
    ground.
              Stand up now, stand up now.

The lawyers they conjoin, stand up now, stand up
    now,
  The lawyers they conjoin, stand up now;
To arrest you they advise, such fury they de-
    vise,
The devil in them lies and hath blinded both their
    eyes.

          Stand up now, stand up now.

The Clergy they come in, stand up now, stand up
    now,
  The Clergy they come in, stand up now;
The Clergy they come in, and say it is a sin
That we should now begin our freedom for to
    win.

          Stand up now, Diggers all!

The tithes they yet will have, stand up now, stand
    up now,
  The tithes they yet will have, stand up now;
The tithes they yet will have, and lawyers their
    fees crave,
And this they say is brave, to make the poor their
    slave.

          Stand up now, Diggers all!

'Gainst Lawyers and 'gainst Priests, stand up now,
    stand up now,
  'Gainst Lawyers and 'gainst Priests, stand up now;
For tyrants they are both flat against their oath,
To grant us, they are loath, free meat and drink
    and cloth.
               Stand up now, Diggers all!

The club is all their law, stand up now, stand up
    now,
  The club is all their law, stand up now;
The club is all their law to keep men in awe;
But they no vision saw to maintain such a law.
               Stand up now, Diggers all!

The Cavaliers are foes, stand up now, stand up now,
  The Cavaliers are foes, stand up now;
The Cavaliers are foes, themselves they do disclose
By verses, not in prose, to please the singing boys.
               Stand up now, Diggers all!

To conquer them by love, come in now, come in now,
  To conquer them by love, come in now;
To conquer them by Love, as it does you behove,
For He is King above, no Power is like to Love.
               Glory, glory, Diggers all!

APPENDIX B

THE CULT OF THE GOLDEN CALF

" And Jesus went into the Temple, and overthrew the tables of the Money-changers, and taught, saying unto them, Is it not written, My house shall be called of all nations the house of prayer? but ye have made it a den of thieves."—*Mark* xi. 15–17.

" In vain ministers preach the Gospel of Peace and Righteousness. In vain Peace Societies are established. The 'Gold Standard' means inevitable war. Nations cannot possibly remain long under it.

" 'The nations born of thee are fire and sword,
Red ruin and the breaking up of laws.'

" It is strange that land reformers are so absolutely blind to this fact. One never hears of money-lords begging for land on which to employ their wealth. But landlords are continually becoming indebted to the Money-power for the use of money. In other words, land is far more plentiful and more readily procurable than money. And to-day money is made more essential to men than land. *And into the hands of the Money-power the land must inevitably fall.*"—ARTHUR KITSON (U.S.A.), " A Scientific Solution of the Money Question."

IN recent times that hardest of all economic problems—the money question—has been tackled by several writers of unquestionable courage and capacity. But somehow we get " no forrarder "

to speak of. Indeed, we require to go back to
the bitter anti-usury struggles waged by the
Plebeians against the Patricians of ancient Rome,
to find anything like a parallel to the calamities
with which the world of Labour is now threatened
by the remorseless and ubiquitous operations of
the Money-power.

Those who have done me the honour of per-
using the abridged Gospel according to Winstanley
the "Digger," will recall the intrepid "Leveller's"
short way with the money-mongers. Not only
in his eyes was "money the root of all evil,"
but the very custom of purchase and sale
he roundly denounced as an incurable "nursery
of cheaters." In his Righteous Commonwealth
the buying and selling of lands, commodities,
or services was high treason in its most aggra-
vated form. But this, alas! is still the day of
small unheroic things, and it remains to be seen
to what extent it is possible to introduce into
the "nursery of cheaters" an innocuous *medium
of exchange.*

The earliest form of exchange, of course, was
barter. One commodity was given directly for
another. But as society progressed, the barter

system was felt to be too cumbersome, and the idea of a *common measure of value* was evolved.

For this purpose sundry "standards" were set up. Among the more savage tribes, at various times and places, skins of wild beasts, flint arrowheads, &c., were used; and to this day in Africa, among pastoral tribes, oxen are money, and, in many parts of Asia, camels.

It was also so in ancient Greece. Homer estimates the arms of Diomed at nine oxen, and the earliest Greek coins are stamped with a symbolic ox's head, in token of "survival."

Indeed, the *media of exchange* have been very various—among them cowry shells, periwinkles, clams, &c. In China the bark of the mulberry tree, in India cakes of tea, in Abyssinia salt, were in extensive use. Sparta had a currency of iron, Burmah of lead, Scotland of nails, New England of bullets, Virginia of tobacco, and Massachusetts of codfish.

But the "classes" at a very early stage of civilisation were quick to discover that all such money commodities were too accessible to the "masses," inasmuch as they themselves could not control the circulation. It was therefore necessary to have recourse to some material or materials that they could manipulate at will—some rare substance, if possible, that could be invested with superstitious reverence in the eyes of the gullible multitude. The kings and nobles accordingly, as they always do whenever they have anything unusually nefarious on hand, called in the aid of the priests, and these pronounced gold and silver, particularly gold, of "divine origin," and as such the peculiar property of the "classes," who were themselves, to be sure, descended from the gods.

Sun worship was the most prevalent form of religion in the ancient world, and gold, it was declared, was "sun-begotten." It was, therefore, both sacred and symbolic. The sun-god was frequently represented by a golden disc or round table placed in his temples, and in that form received the adoration of his devotees. Pindar invokes Theia, the mother of the sun-god, as she "through whom it is that mortals esteem mighty gold above all things else."

And to this hour "mighty gold" has lost none of its fascination for mankind. Not only is the question of the currency pronounced beyond the comprehension of ordinary mortals, but the high priests of the Money-power have proclaimed it political sacrilege even to contemplate the subject. It is *taboo*.

With infinite labour and frequent bloodshed we extract this " precious metal " from certain holes in the remotest parts of the earth, and then hasten with it over land and sea in order, for the most part, to bury it again in certain other holes or bank vaults, whence able editors solemnly assure us that it mysteriously controls the destinies of mankind as the " standard of value." Good old " standard of value " !

Is it possible to conceive of a more debasing *cult*—a more baneful superstition ? The golden " calf " which Aaron, " with a graven tool," fashioned for adoration by the Hebrew idolaters, was assuredly by comparison quite a respectable deity.

" What blasphemy ! " chorus usurers of every strype. " Is not gold *sound* money—the only *natural* medium of exchange ? Is not the face value and the intrinsic or commodity value of the sovereign identical ? "

Very far from it, ye juggling high priests of Mammon ! Demonetise this most delusive of " precious metals " to-morrow, and so far as the useful arts are concerned, it will be an absolute drug in the market for the next sixty or seventy years. It will at a blow lose more than 90 per cent. of its value. That is to say, of £100 in gold, the crude metal will = £10, and the Mint stamp = £90! Nay, if all the gold above ground, minted and unminted, estimated to be worth about £5,000,000,000, were collected together and dropped into mid-Atlantic, the real wealth of the world would not undergo the slightest diminution. Nor is it possible to imagine a more salutary revolution.

But, though the commodity value of gold is of little or no account, the labour required to raise even an ounce of it is almost fabulous. Del Mar, a very high authority, tells us that the £90,000,000 of gold raised in California, in 1848–56 inclusive, cost in labour alone £450,000,000, or five times its mint value!

Ah! but then we are admonished by the worshippers of the Golden Calf that their idol is indispensable, inasmuch as it furnishes us with an " *Unvarying*, and the only *Unvarying*, Standard of Value"! Good old " Un*varying* Standard"!

In point of fact *all* "standards" involving a

commodity value, in the very nature of things fluctuate, and about the least stable among them is gold.   Between the years 1789–1809 it fell in purchasing power 46 per cent., and rose again, from 1809 to 1849, 145 per cent. ; while from 1849 to 1874 it fell 20 per cent.   And now, Dr. William Smart, Professor of Political Economy in the University of Glasgow, tells us ("Studies in Economics") that " a sovereign to-day will exchange for 66 per cent. more of things in general than it did some twenty years ago."

Gold is therefore obviously a very lame "standard of value," and it would never have been permitted to masquerade in that character but for the fact that it is so easy for bankers, usurers, and other *hostes humani generis* to " corner " it, and thereby make the whole world of toil their tributaries.   It is *scarce* and it *glitters*.   Wherefore it is that Shylock is striving, might and main, to make it the sole final money of redemption throughout the world.

In 1873, by a gross fraud on Congress, he succeeded in demonetising silver, thereby practically *doubling* the indebtedness of every mortgagor and other debtor in the United States, and now he is bending every energy to enmesh South America and Asia in the golden net in which he has already hopelessly entangled Europe and North America. If he succeed, the value of his accursed gold will be *quadrupled ;* or, to put it otherwise, commodities must decline to one-fourth of their present price, and labour, all the world over, be reduced to one dead level of worse than Egyptian bondage.

Quite otherwise is it with the ideal or *immaterial* dollar, which is thus evolved. VALUE IS REALLY A RELATION BETWEEN TWO POWERS, A RATIO BETWEEN TWO NUMBERS. Take the following commodities as equivalents in exchange or barter :—

400 lbs. sugar = 50 lbs. butter = 40 lbs. coffee = 20 bushels potatoes = 25 yards cloth = 10 oz. gold. Next, divide their least common multiple by each quantity :—

400

400 Sugar.	50 Butter.	40 Coffee.	20 Potatoes.	25 Cloth.	1 Gold.

which becomes in value form :—

Sugar.	Butter.	Coffee.	Potatoes.	Cloth.	Gold.
1	8	10	20	16	400

Taking 1 as the denominator we thus find that

sugar is 1 unit per pound; butter, 8 units; coffee, 10 units; and so on.

By this means the ideal or "honest dollar" of 100 cents., printed on pieces of durable paper of convenient size and of infinitesimal "intrinsic value" is reached, and the corner-stone of the new system of *Free Mutual Banking* is laid. *Every* form of wealth, gold and silver included, may readily be represented in units or multiples of units of the new money, which can neither by reason of its abundance be "cornered" nor made the subject of usury.   In every case the valueless paper notes are issued against commodities or services pledged for their redemption, and the moment they are returned to the bank the goods are released.

The office of banker might be undertaken or superintended by Parish Councils, District Councils, County Councils, Town Councils, Co-operative Stores, or even by individual merchants.   Such Mutual Banks indulge neither in stocks nor dividends, and the cost of "running" them, it is calculated, would not exceed *three-fourths of one per cent. !*

The existing spider-web system of banking was

not created in a day. It was contrived by Shylock
a little at a time, and has cost him an infinitude
of patient scheming. He opens a vault and
offers to take care of his neighbour's money
free of charge, or even allows him a trifling per-
centage for the honour of his confidence. The
banker's course is then clear enough. He must
keep a safe fraction of gold on hand, so as to be
able to deliver whatever amount any depositor
may chance to call for. But he soon ascertains
both what his "average deposits" are and what
his "average withdrawals," and it consequently
becomes easy for him to determine how much of
his neighbour's money he can prudently keep out
on loan all the while.

And it is amazing what stupendous banking
credits *can* be supported on the slenderest gold
reserves. By recent official returns, for example,
it appears that in Scotland £92,000,000 of banking credits rest on a gold reserve of £4,000,000 !
In Great Britain, at the present moment, the
coin amounts to about £110,000,000, and the
credit forms to £10,890,000,000, *all payable in
gold !*

Of course, many promises to pay in gold may be

made to balance or cancel each other; but that process has an inevitable limit. The production of gold is but a "flea-bite" to the increase of interest, simple and compound. "I estimate," says Michael Flürscheim, whose experience as a banker, merchant, and manufacturer places him in the first rank of authorities, "their yearly increase at over £600,000,000, *which exceeds twenty times the annual output of gold in the whole world.*

"Thus the gulf between the actual money stock and the amount of money-promises widens from year to year, and the risk run by money-lenders widening in proportion, they necessarily become more and more cautious, and lend only on the best security or at extortionate rates. A growing number of people cannot supply such security, or pay the high interest, and consequently can neither obtain the control of real money nor of currency, *i.e.* the current money promises.

"Do you now recognise the nature of the road which leads to the precipice, ready day by day to engulf any one of us? No one is entirely safe; no one can command safety for those dearer to him than his own life. Steeper and steeper

the road descends, and—with every advance in
the arts of production and distribution—faster
and faster do we glide towards the horrible
deep.

"No wonder the instinct of the man of the
people teaches him that this 'progress' is his worst
enemy, though, under natural conditions, it should
be his best friend.   But conditions are most un-
natural when our whole currency is forced through
the needle eye of the relatively small gold-stock.
This must create a terrible struggle for the small
outlet, and the smaller the orifice in proportion to
the increasing volume of trade, the fiercer must
the struggle be.   Progress now means simply a
still more rapid increase of trade, without a corre-
sponding increase in the dimensions of the gold
door through which trade must pass.   Can we
wonder at the hatred of new machinery under such
circumstances ?   If the road leads to the precipice
it is certainly more advisable to ride in a bullock-
cart than in an express train.   The latter would
but hurl us so much sooner to the bottomless
abyss."

The "struggle for the small outlet" is to be
seen at this moment in the Transvaal in its most

appalling form.   Shylock pipes, and Boer and Briton, in responsive frenzy, dance in pools of blood, like the victims of the cruelest enchantment.   The spectacle is enough to melt the heart of a Satyr, or of Satan himself, to pity.

" O Lord ! what fools these mortals be ! "

THE END